The **Paren**Talk Guide to Your Child and the Internet

The
Paren￬alk
Guide to
Your Child and
the Internet

Jonathan and Lucy Bartley

Series Editor: Steve Chalke

Illustrated by John Byrne

Hodder & Stoughton
LONDON SYDNEY AUCKLAND

First published in Great Britain in 2003

10 9 8 7 6 5 4 3 2 1

British Library Cataloguing in Publication Data
A record for this book is available from the British Library

ISBN 0 340 86118 5

Typeset in Sabon by Avon DataSet Ltd,
Bidford-on-Avon, Warwickshire

Printed and bound in Great Britain by
Bookmarque Ltd, Croydon, Surrey

The paper and board used in this paperback are natural recyclable products
made from wood grown in sustainable forests. The manufacturing processes
conform to the environmental regulations of the country of origin.

Hodder and Stoughton
A Division of Hodder Headline Ltd
338 Euston Road
London NW1 3BH
www.madaboutbooks.com

Contents

Acknowledgements

So many people have been so helpful to us while we have been writing this book, it is difficult to know where to start in thanking them.

Perhaps we should begin by acknowledging the great support our own parents have been, not just in recent months but throughout our lives. Then there are our children, Charis and Samuel, who have taught us so much, not just about being parents but about being children too.

The Parentalk team have been particularly patient with us as we have missed deadlines and changed chapters. Sophia Hanvey has been wonderful in reading, critiquing and offering creative ideas on drafts of the book.

Lastly we would like to thank Ben Harvey and Nick Turner, who worked and put up with us at exalt.co.uk, but have also been such wonderful friends.

This book is dedicated to the memory of David McGavin, who founded exalt, but was taken from us so tragically a few years ago shortly after its launch. We look forward to seeing you again one day.

Jonathan and Lucy Bartley, 2002

Introduction

Ian and Jane were thrilled to see their daughter's picture in the local paper. She had worked so hard on her poem, and it was a great achievement to have it judged first in a competition with over 1,000 entries. Brimming with pride they cut the picture out for the photo album and made copies for friends and family. They planned to send it out with the family news in their Christmas cards.

But a few days later they discovered that their daughter's picture had also been placed on the newspaper's website. Horrified, they called the editor. Why had they done such a thing? She was only nine years old! Who knows who would see it? How could they expose a child in this way?

The very mention of the Internet produces a range of emotions in all of us, particularly when our families are involved. Despite the fact that a photograph would probably be seen by many more people in a local newspaper than on its website, stories of paedophiles, pornography, viruses and dot.com crashes echo in our minds whenever the 'I' word is mentioned.

Our parenting instincts tell us to minimise our children's exposure to such things and protect those that we love at all costs.

But the Internet can also throw up a completely different set of emotions. You yourself may be a keen Internet fan. If not, we've at least heard of the benefits that come from Internet use. We probably have friends who've told us that they found this or that useful thing 'on the Net'. We have perhaps seen the adverts for cheap web-based airlines, or listened to the presenter of a television or radio programme tell us about a website we can visit for more information about the subject of a programme. There is no doubt about it – the Internet can be an amazing aid for a range of things, whether it be healthcare, holidays or home improvement. It's only natural that we don't want our families to miss out.

So, we're torn between positive and negative feelings. This book has been written to help you, as a parent, cut through the jargon and the hype, and to enable your family to make good, commonsense decisions about Internet use.

Internet, Internet everywhere . . .

'Are we there yet? Are we there yet?' the children sitting behind their dad yell, as they bounce up and down in their seats and simultaneously peer over his shoulder.

This scene from an advert in the USA is all too familiar. Parents throughout the world identify closely with this father, who we assume is taking the children on a long car journey. However, as the camera pans back, we see that they are not sitting in a car at all. In fact, they are all sitting in front of a computer. Dad is not taking the children anywhere. He is struggling with a troublesome and extremely slow Internet connection as his children wait impatiently to go online.

The Internet can be part of family life in many ways. This is not surprising, given that there are 18 million adults in the UK who use the Internet on a regular basis from home and/or work.[1]

You can now do your weekly shopping online and have it delivered to your door. You can sort out your personal finances, whether it's investments, insurance or personal banking or

HELP! WE'RE
PARENTS DROWNING
IN INFORMATION!

paying utility bills. You can get help with homework and medical problems, play games, pursue a hobby, listen to music, watch films and keep in touch with old friends as well as making new ones. In some areas you can even vote in elections and get access to your MP and local councillors.

Of course, every family will use the Internet to varying degrees and in different ways. But whether you're already taking advantage of the benefits that going online has to offer, or just thinking about going online for the first time, this book is here to enhance your family's Internet experience.

Such is the nature of the Internet that there's always something out there that you haven't heard of or wish that you'd known about earlier. So we've included tips and ideas about how to find what you want and make the most of the websites that people are already using but perhaps you'd never thought about. Whatever stage you are at, this book will give you more ideas and suggestions about how the Internet can be used more effectively as part of your family life.

Keeping your head above water

For some people, however, particularly those who readily admit to having little or no 'Net nous', we recognise that this book will be simply a tool for survival!

What image comes into your head when you hear the Internet mentioned? A personal computer sitting on a desk in your office or sitting room, perhaps? This is an image that most people would share, but it's one that's rapidly changing.

It is now hard to find a place where the Internet is not used in some shape or form. It can no longer be confined to the office or the family sitting room. The Internet is connected to our mobile phones, to our televisions, to our personal organisers. If the prophets are to be believed it will soon be connected to all of our washing machines and central heating systems! The rules just keep on changing, and the lines between what's Internet and what's not get more and more blurred.

But this same rapidly changing pace of technological development can easily make parents feel out of their depth, if not drowning, in a sea of megabytes. They may remember the small personal computers that they played games on as a child, or

EVERY TIME THE KIDS ASK ME ABOUT 'MEGA BYTES' I HAVE TO BITE MY TONGUE..

the little bit of computing that they did at school. The world of the Internet can seem like an entirely different universe.

Throughout this book we've tried to explain terms clearly and simply, and we've thrown out the jargon wherever possible. So if you think a mouse pad is somewhere a rodent lives, a cursor is someone who swears a lot, and a hard drive is a long trip on the road, don't worry. By the end we hope that you won't just feel you are avoiding drowning, but positively surfing.

Something old, something new

The feeling of panic in the face of new technology is nothing new. Parents in each generation have had to face a changing world and deal with its implications for their children. When the motorcar was invented, amazing opportunities for family mobility developed. Family and friends could be more easily contacted and visited. Holidays were easier to take, opening up a whole new world for children.

But as traffic incrcased, fears about child safety increased too. Suddenly, there was a need to educate our children about the dangers of traffic, and, more recently, about its effect on the environment.

The good news is that the principles of looking after children and helping them to develop and grow are the same now as they were then. But the challenge is that, as with most technological developments, we can't bury our heads in the sand and hope it will all go away. Just as parents couldn't ignore the development of the motorcar, we can't ignore the Internet either.

Parents need to get to grips with both the Internet's uses and its abuses – the ways it can help our families and lives as well as harm them. It can be a real asset, but we need to know how to make the most of it. As parents, we also need to know the potential dangers that lie out there – what to be wary of, how to prepare for, or avoid, difficulties and problems, and how to deal with them if they arrive.

The truth is out there

Some people say that the Internet makes it harder to be a parent. They worry about losing control, or what their children might be exposed to. Others say that it makes it easier, as they can contact their children no matter where they are in the world, or help younger children with homework by searching the Internet for information. As is so often the case in parenthood, the truth is somewhere in between.

What should become apparent in the following pages is that there are no quick-fix solutions. There is no super-program that will bring all your Internet troubles to an end and leave you surfing happily ever after. What you *will* find in this book, however, is practical help to navigate your way through the world of megabytes and modems, browsers and bandwidths, networks and netnannies, and make the most of the World Wide Web.

We begin by giving an explanation of the history of the Internet and how it all began. We will answer some of the questions and explain some of the terms that everyone uses (although often they're unsure of what they really mean). We will guide you through getting online and finding what you want online, and the variety of ways that the Internet can be used.

As you would expect from a book on a subject as notorious as the Internet, we will also take a look at the dangers and pitfalls it brings. Chatrooms, safe-surfing options and using

IT'S GREAT THAT YOU AND MUM WANT TO SHARE THE INTERNET WITH ME...

YES — BUT TOO BAD WE CAN'T SHARE THE PHONE BILL.

the Internet responsibly all make an appearance, and we'll go on to suggest ten top websites to explore with your children.

Finally, we take a look at where the Internet is heading. One of the problems in writing a book like this is that things alter so rapidly. Just when you think you understand, it all changes. So we'll have a gaze into the future at what might be around the corner, so you can be prepared.

At the end of the book is a glossary of terms, with simple, easy explanations and definitions which you may want to refer to as you work your way through.

Whether you are a first-time user or a veteran surfer, we hope that this book will help you to have a positive Internet experience with your children.

Summary

- This book has been written to help parents work through the range of issues that the Internet throws up, enabling families to make good, commonsense decisions about Internet use.
- Every family will use the Internet to varying degrees and in different ways.
- The rapidly changing pace of technological development can easily make parents feel out of their depth, but there is no need to panic.
- The Internet can make it both harder and easier to be a parent, but whatever you think of it, it can't be ignored.
- There are no quick-fix solutions and no substitute for sharing the Internet experience with your child.

Everything you wanted to know but didn't dare ask

If you've got young children, chances are you'll have seen the Tweenies. These colourful characters, Jake, Bella, Milo and Fizz, spend most of their time at their playgroup where they're looked after by Max and Judy. In one scene the youngest Tweenie, Jake, is sitting at the computer with Max. They are exploring together when Max says: 'Open the list thing.'

'It's a menu, Max,' says Jake disparagingly.

'Whatever you say, Jake,' says Max.

A scene painfully familiar to parents the world over!

Keeping up with the kids

Whereas with the development of the motorcar, mentioned in our introduction, adults were the first to get to grips with the new technology, with the Internet the tables have turned. About three-quarters of British children aged between seven and sixteen now have Internet access, and the numbers are increasing steadily.[2]

The chances are that your children will know more about the Net than you do. But this means that we can easily feel as if the world is passing us by, and be fearful about what our children might be doing online – an unknown world that we are powerless to enter.

But there is no need to feel out of control. After all, if millions of adults and children can get to grips with the Net, then so can we!

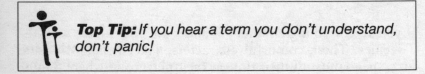

Top Tip: *If you hear a term you don't understand, don't panic!*

US President Harry Truman once said that the best way to give advice to your children is to find out what they want and then advise them to do it! Given years before the computer was developed, there is an element of truth in his suggestion.

The basics of Internet use are simple to grasp and the Net itself can be a great help when it comes to the job of parenting. In an age when parents are supposed to be experts on everything from drug abuse to homework assignments, from your child's school's position in a league table to what to put on the dinner table, the Internet can be a godsend. Never before has so much parenting information been so readily available.

There are other spin-offs, too. Thanks to the Internet there are new opportunities for many parents to work at home and be with their families. We both often work from home ourselves, and have found that provided we lay down clear rules and guidelines about when we are working and when we are not, it means that we get to spend a great deal more time with our children than we would in an ordinary nine-to-five job.

As well as having more access to their parents, children are also recognising that they have access to cultures and new methods of learning in a way that children have never had before.[3]

So it seems that, if our children are already getting stuck into all things Internet, perhaps the best way for us to engage with them is to get involved and learn to use it ourselves.

Attitudes are changing. In a recent survey, half of parents with school-age children said that they thought the Internet was as good as traditional resources for their child's learning.[4] The good news (from a parent's perspective) is that there has been a significant increase in the use of the Internet for exam revision and homework. One quarter of all users access it for exam revision, and this number rises to over half among fifteen- to sixteen-year-olds. Nine out of ten of all users say that the Internet helps them with their learning.

The biggest single factor that seems to affect how people feel about the Internet is simply how much they use it. Similarly, older people who use the Internet are as enthusiastic as our teenagers.[5] One of our friends has a dad who, at seventy-eight, went online in order to keep up with his granddaughter. Now he sends our friend emails that she doesn't even know how to open, let alone produce herself! Parents too need to get online, and when they do the benefits are enormous.

Learning the lingo

Of course, not all parents have children who know more than they do. You may be a regular Net user and know quite a lot about the Internet and its various functions. But while most people talk a good game and speak the lingo, the truth is they often don't know a whole lot more than we do.

For example, how often have you heard the words 'Internet' and 'World Wide Web' used interchangeably? Many people do this. But in fact they're two different terms, referring to two different things.

The web is just one part of the Internet. It is the bit where you can read text, look at pictures, listen to music and watch video, etc. The Internet encompasses a whole lot more.

Top Tip: *You can look up terms you don't under-stand on the Internet. See the next chapter for details.*

In the beginning

A few years ago someone set up a web page that said, in big bold type,

Congratulations, you have reached the end of the Internet.

Of course, there is no end to it, but, as you can imagine, lots of people like to think that they had a hand in starting it!

The Internet began its life in the academic world. The idea was to develop a system where computers could communicate with one another. It was in the USA on the UCLA campus in 1969 that the first Internet connection was established.

But the real precursor to the Internet began with the US Defense Department's ARPANET. The department wanted to create a computer network that would work in the event of a disaster such as a nuclear war.

During the 1960s and 1970s, many small computer networks were created. Some of these networks, called Local

Area Networks (LANs), connect computers over short distances, using cables. Other larger networks, called Wide Area Networks (WANs), connect computers over larger distances, using transmission lines like those used in telephone systems.

But although both local and wide networks made it easier to share information within organisations, the information couldn't move beyond the boundaries of each network. Many of the networks moved information around in different ways, based on their own particular design, and often these were incompatible with each other.

The Internet was designed to interconnect the different types of networks and allow information to move freely, regardless of the machines or networks that people used. It did this by adding special computers called 'routers' to connect the different types of network.

The Internet can be used for a whole range of activities such as sending messages. But it was the newest Internet service, the 'World Wide Web', that accelerated the growth of the Internet by giving it an easy-to-use, 'point and click' style.

There are now millions of server computers on the Internet, each providing some type of information or services.

Who uses the Internet?

We can get the impression that everyone now uses the Internet, but in fact, while almost all Europeans watch television and about half frequently read a newspaper, less than half use the Internet.

Exact numbers are difficult to come by but research suggests:

- One in four British households now have Internet access.
- Two in five people claim to use the Internet at least once a day.
- One in five use it every other day.
- Women are more likely to go online to gather information than men.
- The over sixty-fives are almost as likely to go online to gather information as sixteen- to twenty-four-year-olds.[6]

What does the Internet do?

The Internet, of course, in and of itself doesn't 'do' anything. It is up to you to make it work for you. It is what you and your children use it for that counts.

At one time, the Internet was new and people would spend hours using it just to explore what was out there. It has now lost its novelty value. Instead the medium is now regarded as a

17

daily part of life, and people are generally going online to perform very specific tasks such as shopping or finding a job.[7]

The way that the Internet is used changes all the time, but a league table might look a bit like this:

Most popular uses for the Internet

1 Email.
2 Research, including academic and related research, job-hunting, news and reference and even self-education.
3 Entertainment, including web radio.
4 Banking and finances.
5 Chat and discussion.
6 Experimenting and exploring.
7 Games.
8 DIY web design.
9 Shopping.

Let's look at each of these in greater detail.

1 Email

A husband was giving his wife some space and looking after the children while she took a shower. But after a few minutes he poked his head round the shower curtain and said, 'What should I give them for lunch?'

A bit exasperated at his apparent inability to think for himself, his wife said: 'There's all kinds of food. Why don't you just pretend I'm not at home?'

Getting out of the shower, his wife dried herself, got dressed and sat down at her computer, to find an email saying, 'OK, so what should I feed the children for lunch?'

By far the most popular use for the Internet is communication, mostly through 'email' or 'e-mail'. This means 'electronic mail' and is really a version of the postal service. Type a message on your screen using your email program, enter the email address of a friend, hit the 'send' button and away it goes. The message is zapped across the world (or around the corner) to its destination and placed in your friend's email program on their computer.

Email has many advantages over other forms of communication. Unlike the postal service (known as snail-mail by many Internet users), emails arrive in minutes, if not seconds. It is not surprising that three-quarters of all Internet-connected households use it.[8]

Some of the advantages of email are:

- It's cheap.
- It's fast.
- It's less intrusive than a phone call.
- It's more 'conversational' than a letter.
- You can easily keep a record of past messages.

Email is a great way to keep in touch with your family, as you can also send pictures, sound or film with your email. It has proved particularly popular with parents who have to work away from home, and for keeping in regular touch with grown-up children who go away travelling or to university.

> **Top Tip:** Missed the last post for an important day – a birthday or anniversary? You can now send 'e-cards' which are electronic versions of ordinary cards.

Email has another advantage in that it isn't limited to a one-to-one conversation. Larger email conversations can take place involving more people with 'email groups'. Your email addresses, usually kept in an address book in an email program on your computer, can be grouped together so that a message you send can go to a whole number of people on an email list or group.

To make things easier you can also set up email groups, which are more public. When an email is sent to a specific email address, it can automatically be sent to everyone on a certain list. To respond to the message, others in the group reply to the same address and their messages get forwarded on to the whole group too.

2 Research

It is not surprising that, given the amazing wealth of information on the Internet, a majority of home users use it for information searches and research. Over half of unemployed people using the Internet at home search for jobs online. Just under a third of UK Net users have gone online to access travel route maps[9] before a journey.

When we bought our new house, we found it on the Internet.

Rather than go tramping around estate agents and signing up on their mailing lists, there are several websites that list huge selections of properties for sale. All you do is type in your price range, the area you'd like to live in and how many bedrooms you'd like, and up comes a list, usually with several pictures and extensive property details.

Whether it's finding a job or a new house, or getting help with schoolwork, the Internet comes into its own like few other mediums.

Most of the major newspapers are now online, too. Many people prefer to get a newspaper that they can read on the way to work or over breakfast. But the advantage of the Internet is that news is updated constantly. While the papers give you the news as it was yesterday evening, the Internet gives you the current news. Accordingly, many newspapers now carry on their websites not just the news articles from their paper editions but additional stories as they happen. You can also find out news that might otherwise be difficult to access: for example, up-to-date local news.

 Top Tip: *Most of the newspapers publish their morning editions on the Internet from midnight.*

The advantages of using the Internet for research include:

- the most up-to-date current information;
- the large amount of information available;
- the ease of accessing information.

Particularly applicable is the information available to students. Only 1 per cent of UK college and university students have never used the Internet, according to a study which found that a third of students use the Internet every day, while over half use it three to five times a week.[10] Not surprisingly, a big area of growth is online courses and school research, which is equally popular inside and outside the home.[11]

3 Entertainment

Many people, when they are working at their computers, will switch on a radio or play some music in the background. In years gone by we wouldn't necessarily have thought of using our computers to do it, but that is now all changing. Using the Internet to listen to the radio, for example, may seem like a strange thing to do, until you realise that there are thousands of radio stations around the world and most of them only broadcast locally.

By putting their programming online, however, many of these stations now reach a global audience. Given the amazing choice of radio stations and the fact that listening to them is usually free (although you may have to pay to go, and stay, online), it isn't surprising that one in five Internet users in the UK now listens to radio on the World Wide Web.

The technology that makes this all possible is called 'streaming', which means that you have to download an entire file before the music starts to play. Streaming is also available for video. Although the picture quality isn't usually great (but it's getting better all the time) it does mean that you can watch video clips whenever you like. For example, the BBC now has many of its news reports online, so you can pick and choose between them if you have missed the news. One compensation for the low sound and picture quality is the control you have over the programme. Just as with cassette or video recorders, the video or audio is controlled through a panel, so you can play, pause, fast-forward and rewind at will. What's more, the programmes are usually indexed, which means you can jump right to the part you want to hear: for example, skipping the weather report to take in the local sports scores.

If you don't want to listen or watch through online streaming, another very popular pastime is to download the music or video that you want. This simply means that the information is transferred from a website to your own machine and you can then play or watch any time you like without being connected.

> **Top Tip:** Most new PCs have software containing a media player, which has a radio tuner with hundreds of radio stations to listen into.

4 Banking and finances

With all the hype about Internet millionaires, followed by the dot.com crash, a lot of people are understandably wary when it comes to money and the Internet.

Now things have settled down, many people are finding out that the Internet brings tremendous advantages when it comes to their personal finances, such as

- higher rates of interest from Internet banks;
- easy and wide-ranging comparisons when it comes to quotes on things such as insurance;
- plenty of financial information from different perspectives;
- quick and cheap ways of buying and selling shares and other investments.

Of all online financial products, motor insurance is now the most popular among Internet users.[12] The advantage, as with searching for a house to buy, is that many sites ask you to enter your details and then search dozens of insurers for the best quote according to your requirements.

Over a quarter of Internet users have searched for information on motor insurance – more than 5 million adults. Getting mortgage quotes is also a popular function, since many websites contain calculators which allow you to adjust the figures and your payments and possible interest rate changes, so you can see how your payments might increase or decrease.

Once you have your quote, purchasing is easy. One in five of those who have searched for information on motor insurance have gone on to purchase the product online.[13]

There are other savings that can be made, too. 'Ebanking' or 'e-banking' is short for 'electronic banking'. It is also referred to as 'online banking' or 'Internet banking'. But those are just names for one simple thing.

Ebanking is fast and easy. Everything that you would do in person with a bank teller is done electronically instead. It eliminates the use of paper and replaces it with computer screens.

Ebanking is popular because:

- there's no need to stand in a queue at the bank: all you have to do is log on to the Internet and access your account;
- it's safe, hassle-free and saves hours of time a month;
- you can earn higher rates of interest than most current accounts;
- it is easy to access your statements;
- bill payments can be made online.

In most cases it isn't necessary to change your bank if you want to bank online. Just contact your bank and they will tell you how you can access your account online. However, some ebanks, and most notably the ones that offer better rates of interest, are online only.

Fact:

One third of UK Net users have gone online to use online banking services, equivalent to 5.7 million people in total.[14]

---

5 Chat and discussion

While email is the most popular use for the Internet, some people prefer other methods of communication, which are particularly useful if you want a more immediate private conversation without the 'to and fro' of email or if you want a public discussion where everyone can see what's been said before.

There are two main ways of holding an interactive 'talk' session online in 'real time'.

The first is in a **chatroom**. Internet Relay Chat (IRC) is a worldwide system where multiple users can meet to talk in groups or privately. These conversations occur on 'channels' that are like rooms or specific meeting places. Typically, there is one particular topic of conversation in each place or on each channel. You communicate with other people by typing what you want to say. Other people's comments appear on your computer screen prefaced by the speaker's name or nickname.

The second way is **instant messaging**. Instant messaging is a convenient way to see when friends and family are online and communicate with them in real time. It's faster than email and more convenient than picking up the phone.

To do this you will need to download a free software program that will let you do things like:

- send instant messages;
- share photos, pictures and sounds;
- enjoy free live conversations online;
- access your complete and combined 'buddy list' from any computer you use;
- chat with friends and family or people with similar interests.

Often the screen splits in two. What you type appears in the top half and what the other person types appears in the bottom half. It's not as easy as using a telephone, but it's certainly a lot cheaper.

> **Fact:**
>
> In Britain 16 per cent of web users participate in chatrooms, 35 per cent use instant messaging.

Other methods of communication are **bulletin boards** or **newsgroups.**

Newsgroups are like worldwide bulletin boards, organised around a topic. Some are technical, others silly – and some you don't even want to know about!

USENET is the main collection of over 3,000 newsgroups (discussion groups) where people worldwide exchange information, hold debates and generally gossip. Each newsgroup is dedicated to a particular topic, with names like com.amiga.

LOOK! IT'S A SPECIAL CHAT ROOM FOR TEENAGERS. IT'S CALLED A 'GRUNT, GRUMBLE AND SNAP' ROOM.

games or rec.music.blur. Anyone can 'post' a message on any newsgroup, airing their opinion on a subject or offering an answer to a question asked in an earlier posting. And everyone who reads that newsgroup will read what you write.

A variation on this is a bulletin board (also known as a forum, discussion board, message board or web board). It is probably the easiest way of starting up discussion on your own website, if you have one. It's the same sort of idea as a mailing list or newsgroup, but usually accessible to everyone visiting a given site.

6 Experimenting and exploring

Today you can visit Australia, the USA, Greenland and Nigeria. The bad news is that you won't get any frequent flier mileage. The good news is that you won't need to leave the comfort of your armchair. Such is the nature of the Internet.

While most Internet usage is orientated towards a specific task, just surfing around to see what you can find will always be a popular pastime for some. It is amazing what is out there on the Internet if you know how to find it.

No one knows for sure who first coined the phrase 'surfing the Internet', which essentially means using the Internet to explore what is out there. But there are a number of ways of going about it.

One way is to type keywords into a **search engine**; another is to search **directories** for information. We will look at both these in the next chapter.

A third way is to follow a **web ring**. Web rings are a good way to surf around to related websites on a particular subject. Some similar sites are grouped together in rings and each site is linked to another by a simple navigation bar or link. Once you have visited a site you just click through to the next one in the ring.

Many websites also have 'links pages' which list a number of sites usually related to the site you are currently visiting. By simply clicking on the links, you are taken to another site, which may well also have a links page, and so on.

7 Games

The director of a large company found that many employees were spending far too much time playing games rather than working. He therefore instituted a rule that there would be no playing games on work computers. So he wouldn't be a hypocrite, he had the Information Technology (IT) department get rid of the games on his own laptop.

Therefore, one weekend he was particularly surprised to find his son playing games on it. He asked his son if he had downloaded the games.

'No,' he answered, 'they were already there. They were just hidden.'

On Monday all hell broke loose as the director chided his IT department for not getting rid of the games. 'But,' one of the workers explained, 'I thought I just had to keep them away from you – not from a nine-year-old!'

Not surprisingly, playing games is one of the favourite Net activities for many people – and not just children.

Role-playing games, word games, quizzes, old-fashioned arcade games – the list is endless. Some games you play on your own, some require you to compete with others from around the world!

Games usually require you to download or buy some software in order to take part. There are huge sites entirely devoted to games that show what a wide selection there is.

8 DIY web design

And we don't mean the *Changing Rooms* website! But if you fancy a bit of Internet DIY then setting up a website is something that anyone can do very easily. It is not the domain of professional website designers who charge the earth.

You can now have your own personal website that lets the world know who you are, what you are doing or what you think. It can be devoted to a hobby, a pastime, a passion, your work, your family – absolutely anything.

You may have heard the term '**webmaster**'. This is generally applied to the person who looks after a website. The webmaster will often be the person who creates the website.

There are basically two ways to make a web page. The first way is to create the page(s) on your own computer and then upload them to your **Internet Service Provider** (ISP). Your ISP provides 'webspace', which is where the site will be stored. The second way is to create your web page(s) online using a special program called a Telnet program.

Building your own website from scratch can be daunting, but templates of websites including graphics are now available free online. You can choose the style of website that you want from a selection and then download the template to your computer for your own use. Some ISPs also provide you with sites ready for you to just input your information.

9 Shopping

A man observed a woman at the supermarket with a three-year-old in her trolley. As they passed the biscuit section, the child asked for one. Her mother told her 'No.' The little girl immediately began to whine and fuss, and the mother said quietly, 'Now Anna, we just have half of the aisles left to go through; don't be upset. It won't be long.'

He passed the mother again near the crisps section. Of course, the little girl began to shout for crisps, too. When she was told she couldn't have any, she began to cry. The mother said, 'There, there, Anna, don't cry. Only two more aisles to go, and then we'll be able to pay.'

The man again happened to be behind the pair at the check-out, where the little girl immediately began to clamour for sweets. She then proceeded to burst into a terrible tantrum as Mum again said, 'No.' The mother patiently said, 'Anna, we'll be through in just two minutes, and then you can go home and have a nice nap.'

The man followed them out to the car park and stopped the woman to compliment her. 'I couldn't help noticing how patient you were with little Anna . . .'

The mother interrupted, 'My little girl's name is Lucy . . . I'm Anna.'

Every parent knows how stressful it can be to do the weekly shop with children in tow.

For a number of reasons, our family has started doing our weekly grocery shopping online. There are several advantages, including the fact that you don't have to queue, get in a car or board a bus. When you have ordered what you want, many

31

providers charge about £5 to deliver, but if you have a big family or it is costly to get to the supermarket in terms of petrol, parking charges or public transport it may well be worth it.

Another advantage is that you can keep your shopping list online, see what you ordered last week, and add or subtract items from it. Like a normal supermarket they show the special offers as well. You just make your weekly list, input your credit card details and specify when you would like your shopping delivered – particularly helpful if you can't face going out on a particularly cold day, or you are looking after the children!

New research suggests more Britons are shopping on the Internet. It is hardly surprising when you think that Internet shopping gives access to such an amazing range of products that you wouldn't find in your local high street. One in ten of the population are now shopping regularly online.[15]

- Women are less likely to have bought something online than men.[16]
- Consumers in the UK spend an average of £300 online in the course of a year on items such as CDs, airline tickets and books.
- Those in the thirty-five to forty-four age range account for over a third of all online expenditure.[17]

But just how secure is it to shop online? Security on the web remains a key concern. Globally, almost a third of users who have not shopped online said they were reluctant to commit their credit card details. Many felt it was much more secure buying goods and services in a shop.

Although the proportion of Internet users who feel the

Internet is a secure medium for conducting financial transactions has risen, it has yet to broach the 50 per cent barrier. Moreover, while 45 per cent of Internet users regard the Internet as a secure medium for financial transactions, fewer than one in ten users (8 per cent) believe it to be 'very secure'.

Security is a genuine concern. However, the risk can be minimised by only shopping on those sites that have what are called 'secure connections'. If a site has a secure connection it should be stated clearly both on the main (home) page and when you make your payment. This will mean that your details will be encrypted so that other people can't get hold of them.

Of course, no transaction is 100 per cent secure on the Internet – or in the high street. There will always be fraud. But the simple fact that most banks now feel it is secure enough to allow their customers to manage their accounts over the Internet suggests that the security risk is being minimised.

Summary

- The biggest single factor that affects how people feel about the Internet is how much they use it.
- While other people may use the right language they probably know as much as we do about the Internet.
- The web is just one part of the Internet.
- Fewer than half of all Europeans use the Internet.
- People generally go online to perform very specific tasks rather than just surfing around.
- By far the most popular use for the Internet is email.
- By using the Internet for research you can get large amounts of the most up-to-date current information very easily.

Get yourself connected

A man found himself shipwrecked on a desert island. Sad and forlorn, for a year he lived all on his own, eating bananas and drinking coconut milk. He dreamed of a time when he would once again experience all the comforts of home.

Then, one day, around the corner of the island came a rowing boat. In it was the most gorgeous woman he had ever seen. She was tall and tanned, and her blonde hair flowed in the sea breeze.

As she arrived she said, 'I have rowed from the other side of the island. I was stranded years ago when my ship sank, and I have made my home there. Would you like to row over to my place?'

Together they got into the boat and left for her side of the island. As they approached, he couldn't believe his eyes. There in front of him was an exquisite house, with swimming pool, landscaped gardens and an outside jacuzzi – all immaculately presented.

'Welcome to my home,' she said. 'Would you like a drink?'

'No,' said the man, 'any more coconut juice and I will be sick.'

'How about a cocktail or a cold beer?' she said. 'And would you like something to eat? I have a selection of steaks.'

Trying to hide his continued amazement, the man accepted.

After a short time, the woman returned with the drink and some food, having also taken the opportunity to slip into something more comfortable.

'Tell me,' she purred, 'we have both been out here for a very long time all on our own. Is there anything else that you really miss?' She moved closer to him. 'Something that you would really like right now?'

'Yes, there is, now that you mention it,' the man replied, moving closer to her. 'Tell me, do you happen to have an Internet connection?'

Getting started

A desert island is about the only place that you can't get an Internet connection these days. Since many TVs, mobile phones and handheld organisers can now connect to the Internet, there is no longer only one way of getting online. However, the traditional method, and the one preferred by most people, is via a personal computer (PC).

Accessing the Internet through other means doesn't tend to produce results that are as satisfactory. Although things are getting better all the time, television screens don't show up text as well, and organisers and phones can be very slow and limited. Most people therefore opt for a 'desktop'. A 'desktop' is just a PC with a big screen and keyboard. It is not particularly mobile but can sit on a desk or table happily to be used quickly and easily.

36

Desktops have several advantages for the family. There is usually lots of space in them to store the family files, and they tend to be more versatile in what they can be used for. You can easily keep track of when the Internet is being used, for how long and by whom.

What do you need?

You may already have a personal computer. If so, before you try to use it to get online, you need to make sure that it can cope happily with connecting to the Internet. It is a bit like assessing whether your computer has the right level of fitness. You need to make sure that it is fast enough and has enough capacity to cope with the extra strain you will put it through.

If you call or visit a computer shop and tell them how much RAM your computer has (this is like your computer's short-term memory) and how big your hard disk is (this is like your computer's long-term memory), they will be able to advise you.

If you find that your computer doesn't have enough you can always get it upgraded by adding memory. However, this can often be expensive and so it is usually better to buy a different computer altogether.

You can, of course, plump for either a new or a second-hand one. The drawback with buying a second-hand one is that it is likely to be slow and quite out of date, even if it is only a few years old. Having a slow computer can make your online experience very frustrating. The thing to remember is that computers change all the time. In a year's time, a bigger, faster machine for the same price will have superseded what is a good

machine this year. So if you can afford it, think about buying a new one.

But before you spend hundreds of pounds, there are several questions that you need to ask yourself, such as:

- What do you expect to use your PC for?
- Will you use lots of graphics?
- Will you listen to lots of music?

Think about what your family is likely to use your PC for. This is a great opportunity for a family chat! Is anyone in your family a music buff? For example, if you want to listen to web radio online, your computer must be equipped with a sound card and speakers, or you will need headphones. Do your family take lots of photographs? How old are your children? If they are primary school age or above, the chances are they will want to play lots of games. It may therefore be worth getting a machine with lots of memory, graphics cards and a fast processor.

> **Top Tip:** Buy one or two PC magazines from your local newsagent so you can get an idea of what the various options are.

Choosing a modem

A PC, however, is not the only thing you will need. To get online you will need a modem which enables your computer to communicate and access the Internet via a telephone line.

Many PCs will come as packages with a modem, either inside (internal) or as a box that you attach to your PC (external). External modems usually need to be plugged into the mains in the same way as your computer does. (Some providers of Internet access will also give you a modem – see 'broadband' below.)

The speed that your modem operates at is quite important, as it will determine to a great extent how fast you can access websites, get your emails and obtain the information that you want. The modem speed will be measured in bits per second (bps), and the more the better. It might, for example, be 56.6Kbps (which just means that it can process 56,000 bits every second). This is average, and we would suggest that you don't get a slower modem than this, otherwise it can make your Internet experience extremely frustrating.

Making the purchase

When you have decided which machine and modem you want, it's a good idea to go to a PC shop. You do not have to buy there, but you can see how the machines operate. You can compare the models. This could be a thing that the whole family does. Making the purchase a family experience helps children feel part of the process from the beginning and lets them see the various options for themselves. It might even be that when you are there you discover a feature that would be particularly useful for your family that you hadn't thought about before.

 Top Tip: *It is sometimes worth shopping around a bit to get the best price. Often you can get a cheap deal by going direct to a computer manufacturer.*

Choosing an ISP

Wherever you access the Internet from, you will need an Internet Service Provider (ISP). ISPs usually provide email and web space for a website, should you wish to make one, as well as a way of accessing the Internet.

Choosing an ISP can be a bit of a lottery – there are hundreds of companies touting for business, offering you many different products. There are many offers out there that look too good to be true – and they often are. So how do you know which one is right for you?

 Top Tip: *Ask your friends which ISP they use and what they think of it.*

First you need to work out exactly what your requirements are. Here are some of the things you should consider:

- How much will your family use the Internet each month?
- At what times will you use it?
- How good are you at sorting out technical problems? (In other words, how important is customer support?)
- Would you like to be able to create your own website?
- If so, how much web space do you need to create your own site?
- How much are you prepared to pay?

For the person just starting out, this can be an overwhelming number of questions to deal with. At this stage the decision that you make is important. But don't panic!

The important thing is to set your priorities. Is it cost that is important, your children's safety when they are online, or speed of access to the Internet? Below is some more information about these things to help you decide.

Top Tip: *Some ISPs offer free trials so you can see if their product is the right one for you.*

The bottom line

At one point it looked as though there would never be reliable and affordable Internet access in the UK. Now, however, Internet access in the UK is among the cheapest in the world.

It is, of course, difficult to know how long you are going to spend online if you are just starting out. But you should be aware that there are a range of packages to choose from. With some you pay one monthly charge, which allows you to connect to the Internet twenty-four hours a day, seven days a week, and you won't be charged a penny more. With others you just pay the cost of a local phone call for the time that you are connected. Some packages offer you a combination. To a great extent the package that you go for will be determined by your family's lifestyle. It may be, for example, that no one is around at home to use the Internet on weekdays, so an evening/weekend package will suit you best. To help you choose, these are some of the usual options offered by most Internet Service Providers.

Pay-as-you-go If your family only intends to use the Internet for email and occasional browsing of the World Wide Web, say a few hours a month, then this is probably your best and cheapest option. These services are often misleadingly called 'free'. 'Free' means that you don't pay a monthly fee. But you will have to pay for your Internet phone calls (usually the cost of a local phone call). On the plus side, pay-as-you-go accounts are usually very quick and easy to set up; sometimes you don't even have to register your address. The ISP will just display the necessary access details online or email them to you straight away. If in doubt, this is a good product to start with, as there are usually no contracts that you have to sign up to, so if you find that you are using the Internet more than you anticipated you can easily change to a different package at a later date.

Off-peak deals If you expect to use the Internet fairly frequently, but only in the evenings and at weekends, there are numerous deals that give you unlimited access at off-peak times for a fixed price per month. One thing to note, though, is that life patterns change. What will happen during the school holidays when your children are at home? You could run up a big phone bill if they use the Internet during peak times when you have an off-peak package.

Unmetered access Unmetered access is one of the most popular options. The great thing about unmetered access is that you don't have to worry about the extra costs. If you or your children leave your computer connected to the Internet for a long time by mistake, it won't cost you a penny more. One monthly charge (usually around £15) allows you to access the Internet at any time of day or night, any day of the week, for no extra charge.

There are several things to watch out for with unmetered access, however:

- Performance can be poorer (slower and sometimes difficult to connect).
- The terms and conditions vary – some ISPs will restrict what you can download or place cut-off times to prevent continuous use.

 Top Tip: *It's often sensible to pay a little bit more for a premium service that gives you a better service and fewer restrictions.*

There are also two more options that you might also like to consider:

Subscription There are lots of subscription packages where you pay a monthly fee for both Internet access and your phone charges too. This isn't as ridiculous as it sounds, especially for business users. You often get a quicker, more reliable service with good technical support and other services.

Broadband One thing we would really recommend considering is using a broadband connection, particularly if you use the Net a lot. This gives you always-on, unmetered access at around ten times the speed of a standard modem – sometimes more. Some offers mean that you can also receive and make telephone calls on the same phone line. Some of the best value deals are through the cable companies, but this isn't available in every area yet. But if you are prepared to pay a few pounds more per month, it is well worth it, and will make your time online significantly easier – particularly if you want to perform tasks such as listening to music or watching video.

Top Tip: *Remember – the cheapest price is not necessarily the best deal.*

Other considerations

So far we have looked at cost and speed of connection. But there are also other factors that you should consider, particularly when it comes to the needs of your family:

Web space Most ISPs provide free web space where you can create your own websites whether for your family, hobby or business. But if you do want to create your own website, you need to think about how big your site is likely to be. The things that take up most space are audio, video or lots of photos. However, unless you intend to use such things, the space that most ISPs provide should be sufficient for most personal sites.

Support The level of support usually depends on the amount you pay. Some ISPs only have online support, but others have round-the-clock telephone support. You need to consider how likely you are to need support and at what times. Beware of the charges, though – many ISPs, particularly the pay-as-you-go ones, charge a premium call rate, sometimes as much as £1 per minute.

> *Top Tip:* Call an ISP you are thinking of using and see how helpful they are.

Email Nearly all ISPs now offer multiple email addresses and many also offer web-based email, which means that you can access your messages from anywhere that has an Internet connection. Business ISPs may offer more email services, such as mailing lists. Will you want to access email away from home? If so, make sure that they have web-based email.

Family facilities Some ISPs call themselves 'family friendly'. This means that they will gear themselves towards the needs of families. They may, for example, moderate their chatrooms and supply filtering software and controls for parents. Some people find this helpful, other people find it frustrating as they tend to try and lock you into their services. The best thing to do is find someone who uses a family-friendly ISP and see what their experience has been.

> *Top Tip:* Check whether the ISP has signed up to an industry code of conduct – contact the Internet Service Providers Association (ISPA) for further details.

Getting set up

Once you have decided which ISP you are going to use, you can call them and they will usually send you an introductory package through the post. To set your computer up to get online you just put the CD in your computer and follow the instructions that it gives you.

The process of setting up will include registering, during which you may need to enter your personal details and credit card number, depending upon which package you are using.

Included in this registration process will be the chance to sign up to be sent more information about products and services. It is up to you whether you want to do this. If you do sign up, you can always be removed from their lists later on.

Choosing an email name

As you register you will also have the chance to choose an email name and password. You email name is usually something like yourname@yourisp.com. This will be the address that people use to send you and your family email messages, and so your choice is important.

The chances are, however, that someone else with the same name will probably have already taken your first choice – such as jonsmith@yourisp.com. This is where it pays to be clever and do something a little bit different. You can be very creative in choosing your email address, and there are lots of variations you can use. Often children are the most creative, so you might like to include them when you make the choice.

You might like to consider the following:

- Use a nickname.
- Use your house name, house number or road name.
- Use a variation on the family name (e.g. thesmithclan).

Top Tip: *For security reasons, remember it is best not to use an address that gives away too much detail about you.*

Your email name can, of course, be absolutely anything, as long as it has not been taken by someone else already. However, you will avoid a lot of problems if you choose something that is:

- easily memorable;
- easy to spell;
- not easily confused with another name or word;
- not embarrassing for your children.

Some ISPs also allow you to set up several email addresses, so you can have one for each member of the family.

 Top Tip: *If you don't like the email address you have chosen you can always get another name at a later date and get it to automatically forward all your mail to your new address.*

Going online

Before you start using the Internet it helps to get a visual image of what it is like.

As we said in the last chapter, the main thing besides email, which is like a cross between the telephone and the postal service, is the **World Wide Web**. The web has been likened to a huge library with no card catalogue or indexing system. But instead of lots of books, there are lots of websites linking to each other.

Like a library, each site has an index number. This is a collection of four sets of numbers, each separated by a full stop, e.g. 987.65.43.210. Since these numbers are not particularly memorable, each site also has a 'domain name'. This is a bit like a book having a title as well as an index number. For example: http://www.mywebsite.com.

The ending to the name – the .com, for example – gives you a guide to what type of site it is.

- **.ac** indicates an academic institution such as a college or university;
- **.co.uk** indicates a UK company;
- **.gov** indicates a government site;
- **.net** is mainly used by ISPs and other related companies;
- **.org** is used generally by charities and not-for-profit organisations;
- **.com** is probably the most well known and is used mostly by companies.

It should be noted, though, that these endings are only a guide. People sometimes use domain endings such as .co.uk and .com for family websites.

Your first time

When you connect to the Internet for the first time, you will probably be taken to the 'home page' of your Internet Service Provider. This is the website that your ISP will run, and will probably contain a mixture of news, information about how to get help with your connection, perhaps some games and other features.

The ISP's home page might well be rather boring, and you'll probably be keen to get started and move on. But where do you go? A good way to start to familiarise yourself with the Internet is to type in a web address. You will have seen web addresses everywhere, but the chances are, when you want one, there will be nothing to hand!

Here are the top eight ways in which people find web addresses:

- search engines;
- links from other sites;
- printed media;
- word of mouth;
- newsgroups;
- email;
- television;
- books.

Search engines

Most people, however, don't type in web addresses to get to where they want to go. They usually have to look around for the site that they want to visit. But nor do people want to spend hours surfing around. It can be an extremely frustrating and lengthy experience.

There are two primary ways to search the web: **search engines** and **directories**. Using them properly can save you hours of time, and make your Internet experience far more rewarding.

Search engines are computer programs that index sites according to certain criteria. They use 'robots' ('bots') or 'spiders' to automatically crawl over a site and index it.

Directories offer collections of links arranged into different categories and themes. The directories employ people to assemble their lists of sites. Some also use 'bots'. You can search through the categories and subcategories as you would in a paper directory. There are lots of search engines to choose from, with different formats, such as Ask Jeeves, Yahoo and Magellan.

It should be noted that the boundaries between search engines and directories are now becoming blurred. But as a general rule:

♦ use search engines when
  • you're looking for a particular site by name;
  • you want to combine relevant terms;

♦ use directories when
  • you're starting out;
  • you have a general idea in mind;
  • you want to see what's 'hot';
  • you're looking for the most authoritative sites in a particular area.

NB: *to get the best results, try searches in several different search engines!*

I'M SEARCHING FOR TRAIN TIMETABLES.. BUT THE SEARCH ENGINE'S BEEN DELAYED DUE TO LEAVES ON THE LINE.

Potential pitfalls

1   Search engines are machines. You never know what you might bring up!
2   No search engine covers the whole web.

> **Top Tip:** If you put in double inverted commas in your search, many search engines will search only for the two words together. E.g. "John Smith" will only turn up sites where the two words appear next to each other. If you don't put in the quote marks, any site with the words 'John' and 'Smith' on the page could be shown.

Summary

- Although technology is improving all the time, and the Internet can be accessed from many different technological gadgets, most people still opt for a 'desktop'.
- It is important to assess what your needs will be before buying a new PC.
- Making the purchase a family experience helps children feel part of the process.
- There are lots of different providers of Internet access, offering different options and features. Which one you choose is important and can save you money.
- The World Wide Web has been likened to a huge library.
- As well as index numbers, each website has a 'domain name'.
- The main way that people find websites is through search engines and directories.

Two's company – sharing the Internet experience with your child

A few years ago our family went on holiday to Tunisia. One cloudy day, we decided to take a trip to the local market.

As we wandered around we found that some of the shops were full of junk. Others were full of exciting and wonderful wares. But the thing that struck us most was the keenness that the traders displayed to get us to come over to their stalls and into their shops. They would shout out to us in their broken English as we walked through the market. They made all kinds of tempting offers, sometimes even trying to trick us, or grab us by the hand and pull us in.

When you surf the World Wide Web you are likely to have a similar experience. It will seem as if everyone is shouting at you and wanting you to visit their sites. And like the market, there is a whole lot of junk out there as well as good stuff.

Teaching your children how to discern what is good and what is bad, what to watch out for and what to get involved with, what is worthwhile and what is a waste of time, will be one of the most important things you do as a parent. Nowhere is this more true than in using the Internet, and sharing the experience with your child is by far the best way to do it.

The adventure begins

In every parent's life there comes a time when you allow your children to venture out on their own. You start by taking them with you. You show them safe places to go, and the wonders of the world beyond your front door. Soon you allow them to visit the shop around the corner or the local park on their own. When they return you ask them how it went, and before you know it they'll be old enough and mature enough to go out into the world all by themselves.

It is the same with the Internet. By getting alongside our children we can explain to them what is good, worthwhile and helpful, and what to watch out for. As they get older they can do more on their own. But it isn't until they are grown up that they are finally able to go it alone.

This doesn't mean, of course, that you have to sit down next to them every time they go online. As your children grow up they need to learn to assess what they find on the Internet, and as a parent you can play a pivotal role in helping them to make sense of it all.

> **Top Tip:** Set aside a specific time each week for your children to show you some sites that they have visited and what they have been doing online.

How young is too young?

In France and in many other countries around the world, children often grow up drinking a little bit of wine with their meals, usually with water mixed in, so that alcohol becomes a part of everyday life and they know how to approach it responsibly.

In the same way it's a good idea to help children to use the Internet from as early an age as possible. In fact, many 'One-o'clock' clubs, playgroups and nurseries have computers for young children to use freely. Even if the computers don't have Internet access this is a great opportunity to get them used to the idea of sitting with you at a PC.

Children may be able to move a mouse around the screen from about two and a half years old. Our daughter Charis learnt to type her name when she was three and started to play basic games on the BBC website. When children are very young, you will have to be with them whenever they go online, because they won't be able to do it on their own. But even at a very young age there are activities for children to do on the Internet, and some that you can leave them to do by themselves.

There are some great sites where by just clicking a mouse they can choose a colour and then fill in pictures of their

favourite children's TV characters. You can then print off the pictures so the children can put them on their wall along with their other creations from playgroup or nursery. There are also simple games like snap, where children can help to move a train or car around the screen, or where you can read a story online with them.

Of course, they will probably need a bit of a hand learning what to do, but they can sit on your lap at the computer and you can show them simple tasks. Not only does this give them a good introduction to the computer but it can also help with their hand–eye co-ordination.

Top Tip: *Swap ideas with other parents about what sites they have found for their young children.*

Starting-school age

If they have been sitting on your lap and performing simple tasks from an early age, then around the time that your children start school they are likely to want to begin going online and exploring the Internet on their own a little.

Although they may no longer be sitting on your lap, at this stage you still need to be in very close touch with your children. In fact, now more than ever, parental involvement is key to finding sites that are going to be interesting and helpful.

The crucial thing to bear in mind is that children at this age need to experience positive things. Ideally, therefore, parents need to find sites with activities that can enhance their discovery. Worrying about avoiding dangerous sites can be a red herring. If they were to stumble across something inappropriate, the chances are that they wouldn't know what it was, and it would have very little impact upon them.

The main concern that parents should have at this stage is making sure that children are having a worthwhile and positive experience. The sites that they visit and activities that they undertake online mustn't frustrate them but should make the Internet experience exciting.

At this age they won't be able to use a search engine or surf around, so the best thing is to **bookmark** (see glossary) a collection of sites that they can visit. As you find new and interesting sites, just add them to your list.

Top Tip: Consider restricting access only to sites that you have visited and bookmarked.

Late primary school age

By the time that they have reached the last years of primary school, children are beginning to look outside the family for social validation and information. This is when peer pressure often begins to become an issue for many children. It's also a time when they are looking for more independence.

During these years, children should be encouraged to start to explore the Internet on their own. You can show them how to perform searches using simple keywords, and enter web addresses into their browser to find sites that they have heard about, for example from friends or magazines.

But although they're able to surf on their own, this doesn't mean that parents don't need to be close at hand! Just as you wouldn't send children at this age to a film by themselves, it's important to be with them – or at least nearby – while they explore.

It is at this stage that you will probably want to be thinking about two important issues. The first is where you put the computer – for example, should it be in a family area? The second is some kind of filtering program or software that can help to screen out inappropriate material. We deal with these issues in more detail later in the book.

Time is of the essence

'Cash, cheque or credit card?' asked the cashier as she rang up the cost of the final tin of the woman's weekly shop.

As the customer fumbled for her purse, the cashier noticed a computer mouse in her bag.

'Do you always carry that with you?' she asked.

'No,' the woman replied. 'My son refused to help me with the shopping, so I thought this was the best thing I could do to teach him a lesson.'

Perhaps just as important as filtering software and deciding where to put the computer at this stage is the amount of time that your child is spending sitting at the PC. Some children will have really taken to the Internet by now, and it will be hard to prise them away.

But hours and hours can easily be whittled away online, and for that reason it is a good idea to limit the amount of time that

61

your children spend using the computer each day – although taking the mouse away might not be the best way.

Try to ensure that the time spent on the computer and the Internet doesn't take away from all the other activities that your child could be doing. Children need variety, and it's not a good idea for them to be spending all of their time on any single task, whatever it may be.

One way to deal with this might be through the use of a software time-limiting tool that you can download from the Internet or buy in computer stores.

As your children start to vary what they use the Internet for, time will also become a factor in a different way. They can easily be distracted into playing games when they should be doing research for their homework. It's a good idea to agree limits – not just for the amount of time your children spend online, but for the time that they spend doing particular tasks.

 Top Tip: *Encourage them to explore a variety of websites, not just one or two of their favourites.*

Pre-teens

During the pre-teen period, if your children aren't already doing so they will start using the Internet to help with schoolwork and, perhaps, discover resources for their hobbies, sports activities and other interests, as they want to experience even more independence. Although they might think that they don't really need you any more, we all know the truth – of course they do!

In fact, as they start to use the Internet for such things as homework, you can be a great help in suggesting keywords to search under to find relevant information, or sites that they could try to get the information that they need. Even if you don't have much knowledge of the Internet, as a parent you have a great deal of general knowledge, and that can prevent your children from experiencing a lot of frustration as they try to find what they want.

Projects

The chances are, though, that your children will now want to spend a great deal of time online without your help. But as they begin to assert their independence, it's important not to stop communicating about the Internet and sharing experiences.

When your children are at this age you might want to consider starting an Internet project with them – something that you can do together online. One of the things that is proving very popular is setting up a family website. Some of the things that you can think about putting on a family website are:

- a diary to record key events;
- a family tree;
- pictures, perhaps even video footage – if you have that facility – of holidays, birthdays, anniversaries;
- your family history and origins;

- your family hobbies and interests;
- email addresses of relatives.

But if these don't appeal there are lots of other things that you can begin to do together. Perhaps you share a hobby or an interest. The Internet is also a great way of exploring your family origins. Maybe you could begin to use the Internet to trace your family tree?

One of the great advantages of the Internet is being able to get access to records such as births, marriages and deaths information, immigration records, etc., which can help you trace where your family has come from. There are lots of sites that specialise in helping you to do this. Some of them you have to pay for, others not. There is also free software available to help you, which you can download to set up an online family tree.

Virtual reality

At about age twelve children begin to develop abstract reasoning skills. They also begin to form more of their own values and start to take on the values of their peers. It is important at this age, therefore, to emphasise the concept of credibility.

Children need to understand that not everything they see on the Internet is true or valuable, just as not all advice they get from their peers is valuable. One of the major problems of the web is that anyone can put stuff on it. It doesn't have to be sourced or substantiated. The wildest opinions are right there, alongside the most conservative ones. Pictures can be doctored;

quotes can be changed and misattributed. At least with the print media, books are usually checked for suitable content. In the press there are safeguards that mean people must print corrections if they get things wrong. There is little in the way of similar laws for the Internet.

> **Top Tip:** *Do a search with your children for sites on subjects they know a lot about – for example, a football team or band – and talk with them about the variety of perspectives and opinions that come up.*

At this age your children are very vulnerable to offers and scams, too. There can be a huge range of tempting offers, many of which will seem too good to be true. They usually are! As your children start to use email, some of these offers will find their way to their inbox. Others will come in the form of banner ads on websites suggesting ways of making money, or how they can get 'free stuff', etc.

As your children surf around they will come across many sites which have boxes that they can tick or leave blank to say whether they want to receive further information. This usually means that you will end up on many different mailing lists. Explain this to your children so that they can avoid being bombarded by emails.

> **Top Tip:** Ask your child to talk to you before they sign up to anything online.

Other sites will also make wild claims to be things that they are not, such as 'the number one place on the Internet' for this or that. At this age you can begin to teach your children to think about why the advert, email or site is saying what it is. What is the agenda behind it? Someone wants you to visit their site – but what do they want you to do when you are there?

Many agendas will be financial. They may want you to buy something. Or perhaps they want to find out information about you, so they can market their products. Other agendas will be political – they may be pushing a specific viewpoint on a set of issues. Your children need to be taught to discern what they are encountering and why the various sites are saying what they are.

> **Top Tip:** Visit a few sites with your child and ask them to tell you why they think the site was set up.

Setting boundaries

At all ages, of course, boundaries need to be set so your children understand your expectations and what they should or should

66

not be doing. It's no good waiting for your children to do something that you don't want them to before you make rules. It is particularly as your children start to assert their independence that these boundaries become most important.

It is a good idea to discuss and decide on boundaries together with your children at this age, though. Things that you might like to ask yourself when setting boundaries for the Internet are:

- What kind of sites are you happy for them to visit?
- What kind of things are you happy for them to do online? For example, how do you feel about them signing up to mailing lists and taking part in chatrooms?
- How much time are you happy for them to spend online?
- What tasks (like homework) can they or can't they use the Internet to do?

There is a lot of information in the rest of this book that will help you to decide what boundaries to set. But the important thing is that the boundaries are agreed.

Early teens

By the time that they have reached their teens, children are usually becoming very social. It's no surprise that it is around this age that many are interested in online chat.

We deal with the potential dangers of chatrooms later in the book, but make sure you go over basic privacy rules to be sure that your children understand never to give out information

about themselves or to get together with anyone they meet online without first checking with you. Also, emphasise the importance of never exchanging photographs with people they don't know. At this age they need to understand clearly the fact that people on the Internet may not be who they appear to be.

Top Tip: *Emphasise to your children that, as they cannot actually see the people they're talking to, people aren't necessarily who they claim to be.*

But online chat can also be a shared experience. While your child will want to spend most of his or her time chatting on their own without parental supervision, there are also plenty of online chats that you can share in. Often, for example, after a television programme one of the presenters, writers or actors will go online, perhaps on the BBC website, to answer questions and discuss the content. If your family have enjoyed a pro-gramme, why not go online with your children and discuss the programme?

The sex thing

This is also an age where many children start expressing interest in sexual matters. It is natural for them to be curious – and not unheard of for them to want to look at photos and explore sexual subjects.

During this early exploratory period, it is especially import-ant for children to know that their parents are around and aware of what they are doing. You may not need to be in the same room as your children the entire time that they are online. It's probably a good idea, though, to make sure they know that you and other family members can walk in and out of the room at any time, and could ask them about what they are doing online.

Rather than seeing this as a threat, parents can use their children's interest in sexual matters as a real opportunity to talk to them honestly about sex.

> **Top Tip:** *Think about how you might react if you discover that your child has visited places on the Internet that you feel are inappropriate.*

You can use filtering and monitoring software at this age, but you may start to run into some resistance. We cover the options that are available later in the book, but whichever course of action you choose, discuss with your children why you consider it important. Be honest with your children so that they know what you're doing and why you're doing it. If you use filtering software, for example, take time to explain to them that you are doing it to protect them from material that you consider to be harmful. Just as they cannot go and see certificate 18 films or go to pubs and bars, you are exercising your parental right to stop them surfing to certain places in cyberspace.

Mid to late teens

This can be one of the most exciting and challenging periods of a child's (and parent's) life. Your child is beginning to mature physically, emotionally and intellectually and is anxious to experience increasing independence from parents. This can be the hardest time to make the Internet experience a shared one. To some extent it also means loosening up on the reins, but by no means does it mean abandoning your parenting role. Teenagers are complicated in that they demand both independence and guidance at the same time.

As in all stages of their childhood, it is important that children learn to make decisions for themselves. When setting guidelines, let them have input into them, and allow them to make decisions about how they allocate their time online wherever possible.

This doesn't, of course, mean that you leave them to it. You can be right beside them to help them think through the things that they are doing. Find out their favourite things to do online, and discuss them. Ask them questions, so that they can think about both the positive and the negative aspects of their activities for themselves.

Although it's sometimes difficult to give teenagers safety information, they can often understand the need to be on guard against those who might exploit them. Teens need to understand that being in control of themselves means being vigilant, on the alert for people who might hurt them.

But one of the big problems in the teenage years, as any parent will tell you, is that teenagers want to keep themselves to themselves. Still, they may well experience things online that they would appreciate chatting to you about. For example, if they receive an email that makes them unhappy or someone says something in a chatroom, they need to be able to feel that they can come and talk to you about it. Make it clear that they can come and tell you anything, and you will help them with it – even if they have been doing things online that you have told them not to.

It's important for us to remember what it was like when we were teenagers (although just as important to remember that being a teenager then was completely different to being a teenager at the beginning of the twenty-first century). Set reasonable expectations – and don't overreact if and when you find out that your teen has done something online that you don't approve of. That doesn't mean that you shouldn't take these things seriously and exercise appropriate control and discipline, but pick your battles and try to look at the bigger picture.

If your teenagers confide in you about something scary or inappropriate that they have encountered online, your first response shouldn't be to take away their Internet privileges. Try to be supportive and work with your teenagers to help prevent this from happening in the future. And remember that your teenagers will soon be adults and need to know not just how to behave but how to exercise judgment, reaching their own conclusions on how to explore the Net and life in general in a responsible and productive manner.

 Top Tip: Keep the lines of communication open so that you can talk to your children, and they will recognise that your interest in what they are doing is genuine.

Summary

- By getting alongside our children we can explain to them what is good, worthwhile and helpful, and what to watch out for.
- From as young as two and a half, children may be able to play simple games using a mouse.
- Around the time that they start school, children may want to explore the Internet on their own, but you might want to wait until they are older before you encourage them to do so.
- Discussing and deciding on boundaries with your children about what is acceptable Internet use is extremely important.
- It's sometimes difficult to give teenagers safety information, but most will understand the need to be on guard against those who might exploit them.

Child's play – ten Top Tips to help you and your child make the most of the Internet

There comes a time in every child's life when you have to sit them down and talk to them about the facts of life. It is a time that many parents dread and put off for as long as possible, perhaps hoping that school will tackle it instead!

If – and when – you do get round to it, the dreaded talk will probably seem very calculated, rehearsed and completely out of step with everyday life. You may well sit down and pass on the advice that your parents gave to you. You might dare to offer some slightly red-faced tips. One thing is certain, you don't want to repeat the exercise if you can at all avoid it!

Of course, it isn't just sex that we sit down and have deliberate chats with our children about. At different points we might talk to them about such things as crossing the road, dealing with strangers, driving a car or going to school.

More and more parents are actually sitting down and deliberately talking to their children about the Internet, too – both how they should use it and what they shouldn't use it for.

But ideally we won't just give them 'the talk' and then hope that the issue doesn't come up again. Education isn't a one-off, but an ongoing process. We generally want to share the learning process with our children – provided it's not too embarrassing!

Below are some of our ideas for making the most of the Internet with your children on an ongoing basis. Included are some suggestions about both how to do it and what to share with them. We hope that they will aid you in making the learning process as natural and easy as possible.

Tip 1: Try to make the Internet part of your everyday life

The ideal way to tackle talking about the Internet with your children should be as part and parcel of your everyday life. The good news is that this is becoming easier and easier to do as more and more ways of using the Net are developed.

But if you find that there isn't much that you can share together naturally, try to think creatively. For example, if you're going to cook something, why not use the Net to look up a recipe? You might perhaps decide to cook for a friend from a different country or culture. It's really easy to look up traditional recipes from around the world on the Internet.

One of the things more and more families are doing together online is going shopping.[18] You can shop for pretty much anything, from birthday presents to groceries. If you're thinking about a holiday destination, why not go online as a family and

COULD YOU E-MAIL DAD TO PASS THE SALT?

choose your holiday together? Before you go, look up the location and the weather on the Net. If you're driving somewhere as a family, use the Internet to check the route and the traffic situation.

The key is to get into the habit of using the Internet for everyday tasks. For example, when it's someone's birthday, why not send an e-card as well as a birthday card? If you want to send some flowers or buy a present, why not use an online florist or shop? At Christmas, why not use the Internet to discover how other people in different countries or from other traditions celebrate Christmas?

By integrating the Internet into your everyday life, you stop it from becoming something alien. You can learn the what-to-dos and the what-not-to-dos naturally and as a family.

Tip 2: Take the initiative

As we mentioned in the previous chapter, you have a wealth of wisdom to share with your children. The problem is that they won't always naturally come and ask for the benefits of it! As a parent you'll need to look actively at how you can make suggestions about where they can go on the web to find the information that they are looking for.

It's likely, particularly when they're younger, that your children will not know where to start to look for the information they need. As we've said, having more experience of the world you can be a great help – even if you haven't got a clue about where to start looking for the information that they want, you can suggest keywords for them to use to search with, that they perhaps haven't thought about.

As they get older, you will find that they don't need you in the same way. But when it comes to homework you still have a head start! As your children move up in school, they will increasingly be asked to undertake research projects and more complex pieces of work. Some of this will be done at home – and here's where you and the Internet can really make a difference.

You might like to go online with your children as they start to tackle their homework and help them access the up-to-the-minute news, copies of important documents and photos, and collections of research information that might help them. After all, the Internet can provide everything from weather conditions to population statistics.

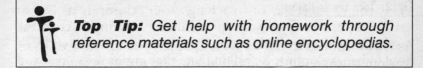

> **Top Tip:** Get help with homework through reference materials such as online encyclopedias.

Tip 3: Netiquette

Most of us learned our manners from our parents. We looked to them to understand how we use our knife and fork, whether it is acceptable to belch in public, when (if ever) we can swear and how to respect others.

ON THE INTERNET YOU'VE GOT TO WATCH YOUR "P"S AND "Q"S ...

... AND YOUR Q-W-E-R-T-Y S!

An old-fashioned term for all this is 'etiquette'. It should come as no surprise that there is etiquette in cyberspace too. Etiquette on the Internet, or 'netiquette' as it is often called, is basically the 'dos and don'ts' of online communication. Netiquette covers both common courtesy online and the informal 'rules of the road' of cyberspace.

Learning together or teaching your children a bit of netiquette can save all sorts of misunderstandings. As in the rest of life, it's well worth taking the time to teach your children how to behave online. By talking together about respectful and right behaviour online, you'll be encouraging your child to be respectful in relationships off-line too.

It is amazing, though, how many people – even regular users – are unfamiliar with netiquette. Unlike the etiquette that is passed down from generation to generation, it is not automatic that you will know about netiquette. There are, however, a number of sites that you can visit that will teach you all about it. All you have to do is type 'netiquette' into a search engine and a range of sites will come up. That way, you can learn about how to behave online along with your children.

Top Tip: Learning netiquette together can be a great way of sharing the Internet experience with your child.

Tip 4: Respect

If you have ever watched *Star Trek: The Next Generation*, you'll know that the crew of the *Starship Enterprise* have to abide by something called the 'Prime Directive', one of the founding principles of the Federation. Basically, this forbids Starfleet personnel from interfering in the development of a less technologically advanced civilisation.

So what's this got to do with the Internet? Well, we have to remember to respect everyone. People learn at different rates and need to feel free to develop at their own pace. Our children need to be reminded that people who don't seem as clever or advanced as we are – which might even include Mum and Dad – deserve the same respect as anyone else. After all, everyone has the same basic feelings, emotions and reactions.

When interacting with others on the Internet, you are bound to come across people who know a great deal more than you do, but also those who know a great deal less.

This knowledge gap may be about technological matters of how the Internet works, or indeed any subject that you discuss in chatrooms or on discussion boards. Of course, there is a place to share what we know. Indeed, this is one of the great advantages that the Internet brings. Knowledge can be shared in new ways that have never before been imagined, but we, and our children, need to remember to share our knowledge sensitively – just because we think that we have something to say, it isn't automatically the correct thing to go ahead and share it.

Younger children can have a tendency to show off. Older children can go through phases of being particularly sarcastic. Some adults can, of course, be just as bad, so we need to set a good example to our children when it comes to respecting other Internet users. The way that information is conveyed can often be just as important as the information itself.

Top Tip: *Ask yourself, 'Would I say this to the person's face?'*

Tip 5: Do unto others . . .

If you have ever travelled abroad, you will know that things which are inoffensive in your own culture can be the height of rudeness in another. In Thailand, for example, it's rude to point the sole of your foot at someone – something that's really easy to do if you have a habit of crossing your legs when you sit down!

When you enter any new culture you are likely to commit a few social blunders. You might offend people without meaning to. Or you might misunderstand what others say and take offence when it's not intended.

Entering cyberspace is like entering a new culture. Certain things are likely to cause great offence, even when you don't mean it. For example, something as innocent as using capital letters in an email can easily give the impression that you are shouting, when you might not be meaning to at all. To make matters worse, as you can't see people in cyberspace, it's easy to forget that you're interacting with other real people.

The golden rule we teach our children is pretty simple: do unto others as you'd have others do unto you. Imagine how you'd feel if you were in the other person's shoes. This is just as important over the Internet as in 'real' life.

Remember to remind your children that although they can't actually see the person they are talking to, they really are there! And just because they are *writing* the words and not actually *saying* them, they are still having a conversation with a real person who has feelings too.

> **Top Tip:** Teach your children to imagine the people they encounter online – it might help them to remember that they are people like them.

Tip 6: Don't jump to conclusions

If you are anything like us, when you get behind the wheel of a car you change into someone quite different. You might scream things at other drivers that you would never dream of saying in any other context. If someone cuts in front of you, you take it as a personal insult rather than a bit of bad driving, and immediately get angry.

People exchanging emails often behave the way others do behind the wheel of a car. They turn into someone quite different, and say things that they would never ordinarily say in any other context. They swear, make rude comments and generally behave very badly. Most of them would never act that way at work or at home. But the machine in front of them seems to suddenly make it acceptable.

When you communicate electronically, all you see is a computer screen. You don't have the opportunity to use facial expressions, gestures and tone of voice to communicate your meaning; words – lonely, written words – are all you've got. And that goes for the person you're writing to as well.

It is extremely important, therefore, to teach your children to be careful about misinterpreting someone's response. Your correspondent will have feelings like you, and it is generally a good idea to give people the benefit of the doubt wherever possible. It is all too easy for a war of words to suddenly break out when the most innocent of comments has been misinterpreted. For this reason, it is very important to teach your children to check that their first impressions are correct before ploughing ahead on a false assumption.

One way of avoiding miscommunication is by using 'smileys'. Understanding and using smileys can go a long way to helping to avoid blunders and misunderstandings. When we talk to people face to face, our body language, the tone of our voice and our facial expressions impart meaning to what we say. None of this is available in the majority of communication online. Tone can easily be misinterpreted or misunderstood. Fun comments can be taken as rude or harsh, and relationships can be badly damaged.

Because of this, an email, discussion board and chatroom language of smileys has been developed to help you communicate a tone. A smiley is a sequence of characters on your computer keyboard. There are now hundreds of smileys that can be used, but there are a few basic ones that most people know and that are used on a regular basis.

The most used is the standard :-) (if you don't see it, try tilting your head to the left – the colon represents the eyes, the dash represents the nose and the right parenthesis represents the mouth).

Smileys usually follow after the punctuation (or in place of the punctuation) at the end of a sentence. A smiley tells someone what you really mean when you make an offhand remark. They are also called 'emoticons' because they intend to convey emotion!

There are literally dozens of different smileys, but few people use more than the very basic ones. Here are just a few to give you a flavour:

:-) Basic smiley. This smiley is used to inflect a sarcastic or joking statement, since we can't hear voice inflection over email.

;-) Winky smiley. Suggests a flirtatious and/or sarcastic remark. More of a 'don't hit me for what I just said' smiley.

:-(Frowning smiley. Implies that you didn't like that last statement or are upset or depressed about something.

:-I Indifferent smiley. Better than a :-(but not quite as good as a :-).

:-> User just made a really sarcastic remark.

>:-> User just made a really devilish remark.

>;-> Winky and devil combined. A very lewd remark was just made – although I'm sure you'll never need to use that one! ;-)

 Top Tip: Why not think about inventing your own smileys to use with family and friends?

Tip 7: Remember that words are written

Unlike a conversation with a friend where there is no record of your discussion, when you communicate online everything is in effect written down and can be stored somewhere.

This means that your words may well come back to haunt you.

We all exaggerate, are economical with the truth and say things in haste that we later regret. Usually, the damage is minimised because we forget or can make amends later. When you post something on a discussion board or send it in an email, it is much harder to retract and sometimes impossible to undo.

Children, of course, are often a bit freer with their speech than adults, so this is a point that they really need to grasp.

Our friend James has a good way of helping his children to understand this, through an email role-play with them. He does this by starting a conversation with his children on email, and beginning a pretend argument.

This is easy to do if you are at work (in your breaks, of course!) and your child is at home, although with younger children you might want to be nearer to them to make sure they understand what is going on. You can do it from the same machine if you have different email addresses. The mock conversation allows you to be a bit provocative in what you say (but, of course, making sure that they understand it is a game!).

Then, a few days later, once the dust has settled, James revisits the emails with his children and re-reads what they sent to each other. He sometimes prints the emails out, as tone can appear very different even on paper than it does on a screen. Together, they see how they sound and what was conveyed in the conversation. They sometimes include another family member who wasn't in on the role-play and ask them what they think of what was said and how it comes across.

Anyone can learn a great deal from such an exercise, and it is a safe environment for children to make and learn from mistakes that in other contexts they might really come to regret.

> **Top Tip:** Suggest to your children that they always take a moment to pause and re-read what they have written before hitting the send button on an email, and if in doubt, to show you.

Tip 8: Remember where you are

The Internet is a vast place, and as you surf around the World Wide Web from site to site it's all too easy to forget where you are. When communicating with other people, it's good to teach your children to get into the habit of asking themselves whereabouts they are in cyberspace. Are they talking to a friend? Who will read what they write? Is it a personal or public forum? Is this the correct context to be saying what they are saying?

The reason is that what might be appropriate in one context can be entirely wrong in another! Teaching your children to tread carefully and be aware of the context that they find themselves in is one of the most important things that they need to learn.

It is, of course, very hard to immediately assess who you are talking to if you don't know them. Some sites are geared towards humour. Others can be 'spoof' sites. Some can be geared towards academics, and others towards children. It's easy to see why what is right to say in one context can be completely inappropriate in another.

Children usually have a harder time understanding this than adults, but you can help them a great deal by continuing to remind them to think about the context they are in.

> **Top Tip:** *When you visit a new discussion board or website with your children, teach them to take time to get a feel for the place before firing off an email or posting something on a discussion board.*

Tip 9: Respecting people's time

If you loathe coming down in the morning to find your doormat littered with junk mail, you will relate to this! Junk and irrelevant mail is a real problem in cyberspace too. Every so often, we find we have to wait about twenty minutes for an email to download, only to find that it is something we have no interest in whatsoever.

It is very easy to send huge files without realising quite how big they are – particularly if you have a very fast connection to the Net. For this reason it is important to teach your children to be careful when they are sending large graphic or music files as attachments to their emails.

Just as infuriating are people who send emails that they think are very important, or funny, to everyone in their address book. It is a very tempting thing to do – not least because, for the sender, it saves time – but it is incredibly annoying for those people for whom it really isn't relevant and something that people soon tire of, particularly if it is repeated often.

Teaching your children to respect other people's time and to be sensitive to their inboxes can save an awful lot of bother!

> **Top Tip:** *Teach your children that what might be very interesting to them is not necessarily that interesting to others.*

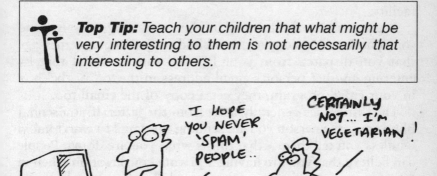

Tip 10: Copying emails

Sarah wasn't home. Her parents were worried and it was getting awfully late. Not knowing any of her friend's phone numbers, her mother went to Sarah's computer and opened her list of email addresses. She sent a note to each name she found asking if they knew where her daughter was. Within twenty minutes, she got back eight replies – all from different friends – saying that she wasn't to worry. Sarah was spending the night at their house and had just forgotten to telephone!

It should have become apparent by now that while email is extremely useful, it is also open to misuse!

One of the most frequent misuses is with the 'blind copy' facility.

A great thing about email is that it is very easy to send someone a **carbon copy** (cc) or a **blind copy** (bc) of any message that you dispatch from your PC. All this means is that by entering another person's email address in the 'cc' or 'bc' box in your email program, they get a copy of the email too.

The difficulties generally arise from the latter. If you send a blind copy, the person you are sending the email to won't know – unless you tell them – that this is what you are doing. People can believe that you are having a private conversation when in fact you are copying your email, and the one that they sent you, to dozens of people. It can be very embarrassing indeed.

You need to explain the principles and different ways of copying online to your children. But there are also a whole load of other things that you need to take into account.

A mother was teaching her three-year-old the Lord's Prayer. For several evenings at bedtime the little girl repeated it after her mother.

One night she said she was ready to pray 'solo'. The mother listened with pride as her daughter carefully enunciated each word, right up to the end of the prayer. 'Lead us not into temptation,' she prayed, 'but deliver us some email, Amen.'

We have compiled ten email commandments which you might like to share with your children.

The 10 email commandments

- Thou shalt not assume that mail you send will only be read by the recipient, and not family and friends, work colleagues and everyone in his address book.
- Thou shalt not change the wording of a message that you are forwarding or re-posting.
- Thou shalt not forward a personal message to others without asking the original sender's permission (before, not afterwards).
- Thou shalt not respond to any message until you are sure it was directed to you, and leaving at least three seconds between the time you first read it and then hitting the send button.
- Thou shalt not forget to check that an address to which you are replying is a single person, not an email group.
- Thou shalt not send unsolicited junk mail.
- Thou shalt not harass a person to reply to an email when you only sent it an hour ago. (Remember that people with whom you communicate are located across the globe. The person receiving it might be at home asleep when it arrives.)
- Thou shalt not forget that the recipient is a human being whose culture, language and humour may have different points of reference from your own.
- Thou shalt not use upper case UNLESS YOU WANT TO LOOK AS IF YOU ARE SHOUTING.
- Thou shalt not use 5,000 words when 50 will do.

Summary

- The ideal way to tackle talking about the Internet with your children should be as part of everyday life.
- Parents have an important role to play in making suggestions about where children can go on the web to find the information they are looking for.
- Learning together or teaching your children a bit of netiquette can save all sorts of misunderstandings.
- Children need to learn that the way information is conveyed on the Internet can often be just as important as the information itself.
- A good way of avoiding miscommunication is by using smileys, or emoticons.
- Children can be a bit free with their speech, so they need to understand that what they write or say online can have serious implications.
- It is important that children learn to think about where they are on the Internet and respect other people, who will come from diverse backgrounds.

Brave new web

The businessman dragged himself home and barely made it to his chair before he dropped, exhausted.

His sympathetic wife was right there with a tall cool drink and a comforting word.

'My, you look tired,' she said. 'You must have had a hard day today. What happened to make you so exhausted?'

'It was terrible,' her husband said. 'The computer broke down and we all had to do our own thinking.'

Of course, we are not quite at the stage where computers do all the thinking for us, but we are certainly becoming increasingly dependent upon them.

While it's really important that our kids learn to deal with the Internet wisely now, it's likely to be even more important in the future. Technological advances will continue to change family life for years to come. This chapter is here to get you thinking about the future, and is something for you to keep in your head while we're talking about how to teach our children to be clued-up Internet users.

It's difficult to predict the future at the best of times. It would take a clever – and indeed brave – person to describe what the world will look like in ten years' time and get it right: such a feat is even beyond the capabilities of Mystic Meg!

Having said that, we can have a look at some of the trends that are happening, to get at least a general idea of where the world is heading. We can look at patterns in technology to get an idea of how the Internet might develop, too, and so understand some of the issues that we will have to face as parents in the future – in the shape of both new opportunities and new difficulties.

The temptation when thinking about our children and the Internet is just to focus on the situation in the here and now. But technology changes so quickly that it's important to look at the issues that are likely to arise in the next few years – we don't want to get left behind! After all, when today's teenagers were starting primary school, there was no Internet to speak of at all – at least, not in the way we think of it now. But if we'd known what was to come, perhaps we could have started to teach them some of the skills and give them some of the knowledge that would come in very handy now.

Those of us with children who are just starting to explore the Internet will, in a few years' time, have teenagers who will also have to grapple with a rapidly changing world. We have to try to second-guess the kinds of things that children will encounter in order to prepare them for what they might face. If we wait until the issues do come up, then they won't be prepared – and nor will we.

> **Top Tip:** *Why not take a moment to imagine with your children what the world might be like in ten years' time?*

The end of the wires

At the moment it's easy to feel as if we're struggling under a huge mound of wires when it comes to our personal computers. There's one cable for this, a plug for that and a socket for something else. Every new piece of equipment seems to bring an additional connection to clutter up our office or living room.

But wires may soon be a thing of the past! **Mesh radio** technology is being developed to deliver fast **broadband** services that are already available through our phone lines. The aim is to deliver high-speed connections to those outside the reach of existing networks.

Mesh radio works by forming a network of users. Each household receives a small radio antenna that transmits on to the neighbouring user – cutting out the need for large antennae or masts.

Even 35,000 feet in the air, travellers on several airlines are being offered the chance to surf the Internet and send email in pilot projects (excuse the pun!). The technology is being installed on aircraft after research found that 75 per cent of business travellers take their laptops on board. It is expected that this technology could also pave the way for streaming audio and television content soon.

This new technology will make our Internet experience much less clumsy, but it will also bring a new freedom. This, in itself, as we shall see, brings with it big challenges for parents, who could be in danger of losing a degree of control, as they try to ensure that their children have the best possible Internet experience.

The Internet in everything!

There are, of course, already developments in technology along these lines that we live with everyday. Internet connections are being included in mobile phones in the form of **WAP** technology, as well as in personal organisers, meaning that the Internet goes with us as we move around. You can now take pictures with your mobile phone and then send them to friends. You can download music on the move and listen to it as you travel. You can word-process on your personal organiser on your way to work and send the document attached to an email to colleagues before you arrive.

MY 'PAPERLESS OFFICE' IS SOMEWHERE UNDER ALL THAT PRINTER PAPER...

Although most people use PCs to get on the Internet now, this won't necessarily be the case in a few years' time. We are likely to see more powerful, faster, all-in-one devices that act as phones, personal organisers, word processors, TVs, cameras, radios, music players and World Wide Web browsers – all hooked up to the Internet. They'll go with us wherever we go.

But it won't just be these kinds of devices that connect to the Internet. Lots of everyday household equipment will, too. The lines between TV, radio and computers have already become blurred. Through digital TV you can already use email services, do online shopping and access the World Wide Web.

Soon, everything from your car to your refrigerator may also be connected to the global network, communicating with each other wirelessly.

Electrolux, best known for its vacuum cleaners, has developed the 'Screen Fridge', an Internet icebox that manages your food, among other things. As you use up the contents of your fridge, it emails a shopping list to your local supermarket and co-ordinates a convenient delivery time with your schedule! The same principle can be applied to other household appliances. A washing machine connected to the Internet could order extra washing powder when it's running out!

Brave new world

The world that our children will grow up in will be one where a time when there was no Internet will seem slightly foreign. The Internet will be so entwined with our lives that it will one day be hard to imagine a world without it.

The second thing to remember is that it has the possibility of giving us more control over our lives and the lives of our children. When away from home, at work or on holiday, we may well be able to regulate our central heating, re-set our alarms if they go off, and turn our lights on and off. It can help to make our lives a more ordered place. Lucy was once sent a birthday card with a cartoon of Dot – a wacky neurotic – jumping out of an aeroplane because she was worried she hadn't turned the iron off before going on holiday. We can all relate to that – but one day, rather than jumping out of a plane, Dot may just be able to press a button to relieve her of her panic.

The implications and possibilities are tremendous and exciting. But at the same time there will also be new challenges – particularly when it comes to helping and supervising our children.

Internet safety

At one level, with the Internet in everything and access to the Internet available everywhere, you probably won't have to make decisions like whether you let your children have a PC in their bedrooms or not. If they have little hand-held devices in their pockets with TV, radio, a phone, email and access to the World Wide Web, then Internet access will no longer be confined to any particular space within the home – they'll have it with them all the time.

Clearly, it will also become more difficult to monitor what our children are seeing, hearing and doing. It's more likely, then, that questions of safety will focus more around filtering software and ways of regulating what our children can access. We'll have to give more thought to what restrictions to place on the technology that they do have, rather than where that technology is kept.

Of course, filtering software and solutions for better monitoring and regulating what our children are able to access through the Internet (which we'll talk about in Chapter 8) will get better and better and more and more effective. But, at the same time, so will people's abilities to find the loopholes.

Making sure we get alongside our children, help them, educate them and learn together with them will, therefore, become even more important in the future. Teaching them to be safe by not giving out personal information, for example, becomes all the more important if we're not able always to be there with them. Their Internet education will need to start from as early an age as possible so children understand the principles that they can apply as the technology develops, and the parents' role in this will become crucial. We'll talk about the practicalities of how to do this later in the book.

Technological dependency

But will these things also lead to an increasing and unhealthy dependence upon technology to run our lives?

Parents are already concerned that their children spend too much time in front of a screen and not enough out developing their social skills and doing more 'healthy' activities such as sport. Certainly, the increase in television viewing and now Internet usage over the last few decades has been linked to the increased obesity in children, lessening social skills and even causing health problems.

Worries about children staring at a screen all day are nothing new, then. The fact that it is television as much as the Internet that seems to have had this effect makes it clear that the problem has existed for years. But there is an important difference. The Internet allows two-way communication in a way that the TV doesn't. Rather than passive viewing, the Internet provides better opportunities for stimulation and interaction.

As with any new technology, it's what you do with it that's all important. The main focus of our attention as parents should, therefore, perhaps be on the new skills that our children will need to develop in order to thrive in the advancing technological environment.

In the information age, one such skill will be managing the flow of information that will no doubt bombard them. Choice can be a liberating thing, but it can also be constraining when you find yourself faced with so many options that you can't handle them all.

Imagine a newspaper that's updated continually with the latest news, twenty-four hours a day, seven days a week. It's been suggested that it might not be long before we find our normal newspapers replaced by a flat panel display of a similar size. The same weight as a few sheets of paper and flexible enough to be folded up to a smaller size when you want to carry it around, your paper would be constantly changing as the news happened.

Just as you can with a newspaper, you would be able to take the screen anywhere with you – even to the toilet. But it will no longer be something that is produced just once a day at breakfast time (by which time much of the news is no longer news anyway). Rather, it will be something that is automatically updated with the latest headlines every minute.

Will the traditional reading of the news on the bus into work, or over breakfast, still continue? Standard routines may well be changed by the new technology, as information is no longer limited to specific times.

The opportunities will be more present now than they ever were, so the importance of being able to discern and take those opportunities is paramount, as are such things as time management. When your environment does not fix your routine, you need to have the skills and discipline to establish it for yourself. There's no way that you'd be able to keep up to date with all the news as soon as it's made public – you'd have no time to do anything else!

The way we work

One of the most amazing ways we are likely to see our lives and routines change is through the way that we work. More and more, parents are able to work from home, or at least bring their work home with them. The boundaries between home and workplace are becoming more and more blurred. This is a trend that looks set to continue. In many ways this can be very positive. It can mean increased flexibility for some parents, who might be able to work from home and so spend more time with their children. But it also means that working hours can change and bring increased pressure as work intrudes upon family life. As parents who work from home, we have to be very careful that work doesn't spill over into family time.

With the post-war revolution in technology, which made new domestic appliances like the washing machine and the vacuum cleaner available to so many people, it was predicted that women – who traditionally were the ones who did the housework – would be liberated. They would have more time, with these labour-saving devices. But what actually happened was that many women tried to fit more housework into the same amount of time. New technology meant that they got more done, but had little extra time to do anything else. As parents we need to be careful that the same doesn't happen with the Internet and our family life.

Rather than giving us more time, working at home could have the reverse effect. It would be all too easy for our time to be further filled with new work commitments as expectations increase, too.

The days of being able to come home and leave our work behind us may be disappearing, at least in certain professions. But with access to the Internet from our mobile phone and email when we're on the move, we can be contacted at any time, wherever we are, even if we're abroad. Work can too easily expand to fill every available moment, which may endanger our relationships with our children.

Top Tip: Set aside regular, specific times for your children and family, on which you are not going to let your work encroach.

The way we learn

As we have seen, developments in the Internet mean significant changes in the way that our children learn. Already, it's not just writing but typing skills that our children need to develop during their childhood. Familiarity with a keyboard may soon be almost as much a feature of education as familiarity with a pen.

Rather than writing becoming useless, it's more likely we'll use a combination of voice recognition, touch and handwriting skills that our children need to develop. If the new technology takes off we may all be dictating letters and emails into our handheld devices. We might want to write on the screens, instead of typing. Versatility and the ability to speak as well as write and type clearly could be important skills for our children to learn.

New technology also means ever-increasing choice in what children learn. Many distance-learning courses, based around

NO YOU CAN'T GET OFF GAMES BECAUSE YOUR TYPING FINGER HURTS..

BUT I'VE GOT AN E-MAIL FROM MY PARENTS...

the Internet and operating through resources provided by email and on websites, are growing in popularity. A huge range of subjects to study is available, if our children are prepared to think more widely and creatively. Again, the ability to make shrewd choices could stand them in very good stead.

Money matters

Inevitably there are financial implications, too. While what was 'hot' last year can usually be snapped up for peanuts this year as technology improves quickly, there are still large pressures on parents to come up with the goods. All parents want the best for their children, and as accessing the Internet becomes more and more a part of your child's education, getting him or her decent equipment on which to work will be less about fashion and playing the latest games and more about good educational tools to give your children a good start. Fortunately, given the competition between suppliers of new technology and the importance of affordability for big sales, it's unlikely that the prices of new technology will go through the roof. However, it will at the very least face parents with important decisions about how to budget for equipment, as Internet access becomes more important within education and daily life.

There will also be considerations stemming from the way that the Internet is likely to be linked to the transfer of money. It is quite possible that we might soon carry around little hand-held devices with us, which we could use to pay for things the way we use credit cards for online purchasing at the moment. Put simply, there will be a flow of money across the Internet as well as content (information) and services (online shops). So when you bought your newspaper or ordered your washing powder, your bank account or credit card would automatically be debited with the appropriate amount.

As money, credit and technology all come together, so it becomes more and more important to teach children the value of money and how to budget effectively. While children may not be allowed credit cards, there's no reason why they shouldn't soon have a kind of debit card built into their hand-held devices, so that when they go to the corner shop to buy their sweets, the money is deducted via the Internet connection in their pocket, and no money changes hands.

As we all know, children have a hard time getting a handle on the value of money at the best of times. It is perhaps even harder when all you see are numbers on a screen. So the importance of teaching your children about the value of money and responsible finances will become even more important as less and less cash actually gets handed over.

Conclusion

Whether your view about what the Internet will bring us in the future is positive or negative, there are some important developments for which we need to prepare both ourselves and our children. The Internet is here to stay. It is changing our lives and it will continue to do so for years to come. It is our children who will face this brave new world, even after we have gone.

Summary

- Technological advances will continue to change family life and the world beyond our front doors for years to come, and we need to prepare our children as best we can.
- Wireless technology will bring a new freedom, but may mean that parents have less control over when and where their children access the Internet.
- When our children grow up, a time when there was no Internet will be hard to imagine.
- Internet education will need to start from as early an age as possible so children understand the principles that they can apply as technology develops.
- Children will need to develop important skills such as typing and how to manage large amounts of information and money which they can only see on a screen.

So far, so good

On a flight to Florida, an educational psychologist was preparing her notes for a parent-education seminar she was about to give upon her arrival.

Spotting the notes, an elderly woman sitting next to her explained that she was returning to Miami after having spent two weeks visiting her six children, eighteen grandchildren and ten great-grandchildren in Boston.

'What do you do for a living?' asked the elderly woman.

'I'm an educational psychologist,' came the reply.

Sitting back in her seat and picking up a magazine, the elderly woman said, 'Well, if there's anything you want to know, just ask me.'

It should have become clear by now that there is no substitute for sharing the experiences with your child when it comes to parenting and the Internet. No expert advice will ever be an alternative to learning with, and indeed from, your children.

So far we've focused on the positive aspects of the Internet, how to get alongside and help your child, what you can do together and how it can be a great asset to your family life.

However, as we saw in the last chapter there are certain things that every responsible parent needs to watch out for. Just as your children have to learn to be careful with something useful but also potentially damaging, like a pair of scissors, they need to understand and be aware of the dangers of the Internet. And just as you explain to your children that they shouldn't run with scissors and must keep the points face down, so there are helpful tips and guidelines you can give them to minimise the risks of the Internet and make sure that the worst doesn't happen.

There's no need to be alarmed by the things outlined in this chapter. The vast majority of people have a very positive Internet experience and never run into more than one or two of the things that we will mention. But as every parent knows, the best way to make sure your children are protected is to be aware of what might happen.

MUM! I'VE SEEN SOMETHING HORRIBLE ON THE NET... YOUR OLD SCHOOL PHOTOS ON "FRIENDS REUNITED!"

Four things to watch out for

As we've said, it sometimes pays to be a little pessimistic. This section will help you understand some of the things that could happen to your children, so you can help make sure that they don't happen. When it comes to the Internet, the basic things to watch out for can be divided up into four main categories:

1 inappropriate information;
2 privacy issues;
3 financial issues;
4 cyberpests.

We will consider them each in turn, not to alarm you but just to help you to be clued up about what could go wrong. In the next chapter, we'll go on to consider what you can do to minimise the risks that your children face.

Hazard 1: Inappropriate information

As a parent, you probably know better than anyone what's going to distress your children. Of course, what might be disturbing to one child may well have little or no effect on another. But overall it has been suggested that one in ten young people have seen something on the Internet that upset or embarrassed them.[19]

In one way this is good news. Most children may never be distressed by what they find online at all. In fact, most inappropriate material will probably provoke curiosity more than any other emotion. But for a minority of children what they find can cause some difficulties, such as nightmares or prejudices, and may twist the way that they see certain things.

The first thing that probably springs into your mind when you think of unsuitable material to watch out for on the Internet is pornography. But there are other things that you need to be aware of. There are other sorts of material that you probably won't want your children to encounter – at least until they are old enough to deal with it maturely.

Some websites and postings on discussion boards, for example, contain hate and intolerance, directed at certain groups. Some sites display frightening or gory images. There are even sites set up to tell people how they can cause harm and make dangerous devices such as weapons and bombs.

As we've said, these things are far from typical when it comes to what you find on the Net, but it is important to watch out for a range of different types of inappropriate material rather than just one or two.

> **Top Tip:** Why not initiate a discussion with your children about what sort of material they think is inappropriate, and see how your views compare?

Another thing to remember is that what your child thinks might damage them isn't necessarily what *will* damage them. And just because they don't seem distressed, it doesn't mean that they haven't encountered something you'd consider unsuitable and potentially damaging online. Of course, what one parent considers to be unsuitable for their children to see will be different from another's view and will depend on the child, so it's important that you make your expectations clear to your child about what you're happy for them to see and what you don't want them looking at and reading. Lay down clear house rules or guidelines, and make it clear when they apply. For example, do they apply when they are at their friends' houses as well?

Remember, there are two ways that your children may encounter inappropriate material on the Net. The first is by accident. The second, although we don't always like to admit it, is by seeking it out deliberately!

Top Tip: *Make it clear to your child that they can always come and talk to you about anything that they have encountered on the Net, whether they found it by mistake or deliberately.*

Oops – what's that, then?

One study of Internet safety suggests that a quarter of children between the ages of eight and seventeen have accidentally accessed pornography while online.[20] There are a number of ways that children can come across inappropriate information by mistake, but here are three of the most common:

Adverts One of the problems is that even on child-orientated sites there may be adverts for websites that you don't want children to visit. For example, children are quite often exposed to adverts for online gambling. Some ads can also be misleading and not reveal exactly what kind of site they're linking to. They might ask an interesting question and urge the child to click on a link to find the answer. A simple click on the advert, however, can take them somewhere that they didn't expect to go at all.

Top Tip: *If you know of sites that your children visit regularly, pay them a visit to see whether they contain advertising, and if so, what kind.*

Emails Children may also occasionally receive emails encouraging them to visit inappropriate sites, usually porn sites. Often, all they have to do is click on a link contained in the email. People may get hold of their email addresses from Internet discussion boards and email them at random, hoping that they will visit a particular site. Your email address can, for example, be taken from an Internet discussion board, and you will be emailed at random with the hope that you will visit their site. Spam, or junk email, is becoming a bigger and bigger problem. It is estimated that as much as 15 per cent of email is Spam.[21]

Top Tip: *Encourage your children to tell you about any messages they receive from people they don't know.*

Internet searches As we've seen already, a search for a certain word can bring up results that aren't exactly what you had in mind. Most of the time, you'll only really find out what a site is about once you arrive there. Doing a search using the name of a pop star, movie star or model might bring up their home page, but it could also bring up sites where they are featured naked! Other unsuitable sites also try and hide behind seemingly safe names such as 'Disney' or 'Barbie', so it's always good to be aware that even what might seem like the safest of searches can bring up surprising results.

Aha! That's what I was looking for!

Of course, children are naturally inquisitive. So don't be alarmed if they're interested in exploring sexual or inappropriate material. Remember what you were like when you were their age! The chances are you did your own fair share of exploring and you probably came through it relatively unscathed!

But how you manage their curiosity will depend on your own view of this type of material. It's important to be aware that some of the materials they might find on the Internet are different from and more explicit than some of the magazines that may have been around when you were that age.

> **Top Tip:** Talk through with your children what kind of sites you are happy for them to visit and search for.

There's a range of inappropriate material that children might come across:

Pornography

Of all the unsuitable material on the Net, children are most likely to encounter pornography. Many children will already have seen magazines on the top shelf of newsagents, or come across it on late-night TV. The first thing to grasp about porn on the Internet, though, is that it can be more disturbing and explicit than anything your children would have encountered elsewhere. Hard-core pornography can sometimes be posted on sites in countries where there aren't strict regulations. But this means that people in this country, including children, can still access it.

Having said that, though, most pornographic sites are regulated up to a point, and some ask visitors to prove that they are

over eighteen. Others ask you to register to access them, and charge a subscription, which will prevent many children from gaining entry.

Top Tip: If your children are old enough, why not take the opportunity to discuss pornography on the Net when you're talking to them about relationships with the opposite sex?

Upsetting images

There are some websites that are set up deliberately to show gory or shocking images. Older children often take a ghoulish pleasure in these and even swap the addresses of these sites with their friends. The images might be real pictures of horrific accidents, images that show disfiguring medical conditions or even images that are doctored to create a shocking picture.

Top Tip: Encourage your children to distinguish between reality and fiction, and remind them that the images that they see on the Internet can often be manufactured.

When they start to play online games, too, it is also possible that children will encounter ones with disturbing images. It's important to be aware of what your kids are doing on the computer, as you may feel that the content of some of the online games that they play is not appropriate. Of course, this goes for computer games even when they're not played over the Internet.

> **Top Tip:** *Play some games with your children on the computer and get them to show you the different games they are playing.*

Hoaxes

Imagine the scene. Your child is doing research for a school project and comes across a website about the destructive chemical dihydrogen monoxide, found in acid rain.

Apparently the chemical can cause excessive sweating and vomiting, as well as severe burns in its gaseous state. Accidental inhalation of the chemical can even kill you. It contributes to erosion and decreases effectiveness of automobile brakes. It has also been found in tumours of terminal cancer patients.

It sounds quite plausible, doesn't it? It should do, because it is all true. The only thing is, 'dihydrogen monoxide' is in fact just water.

Inevitably, sometimes deliberate hoaxes are created, designed to mislead people. In this case, a student at Eagle Rock Junior High School won first prize at the Greater Idaho Falls Science Fair for attempting to show, through a hoax science project, how conditioned we have become to alarmists practising junk science and spreading fear of everything in our environment.

Some hoaxes are just jokes and pranks – but others are malicious and have serious consequences.

In addition to websites, many hoaxes will arrive by email. We once received an email telling us that we might have been sent a virus. It contained detailed instructions about how to check by searching our computer for a particular file. We were then instructed to delete the file when we found it. We duly did so. But the file was actually an important part of our computer software that was needed for it to work properly.

The email was sent to us by a friend who had also been taken in by the hoax, believing that he too had received the virus!

Top Tip: There are websites dedicated to exposing hoaxes, which will give you an idea of what is false and what is true. These sites can easily be found by typing 'hoax' into an Internet search engine.

Dangerous information

We've all heard the stories of people like David Copeland who received six life sentences after being found guilty of causing explosions in Brixton, Soho and on Brick Lane. Soon after his arrest, it was discovered that he'd constructed crude explosive devices using information from the Internet that he'd found after feeding the word 'bomb' into search engines. You probably won't need to worry about your children making bombs, but as parents we do need to be aware that children could be encouraged to experiment with other dangerous information – for example, on how to get high, legally and illegally, and make your own drugs.

 Top Tip: *Working with your child on a science project can be a good way of keeping up to date with what your child knows, as well as being educational.*

Hatred and intolerance

Sadly, there are a lot of sites on the web dedicated to prejudiced and intolerant views of the world. They may be racist, bigoted or just plain malicious. Some sites are geared against a whole nation, society or group of people, others just attack one particular person.

Top Tip: *Why not talk to your children about these sites if they come across them? They might be a good starting point for talking about prejudice and racism.*

Hazard 2: Invasion of privacy

You have probably seen the old Western films where an Indian tracker traces the faintest of trails left by someone trying to get away. They seem to be able to deduce the most amazing information from just the smallest of clues, such as a footprint or broken twig.

When you walk around any website, although you may not realise it you may be leaving 'cyber footprints' behind you. In the same way as an Indian tracker might be able to gain an idea of who you are and what you're doing, these footprints can be used to gather information about you, such as the sites you've just been visiting, what kind of web browser you are using, your IP address (see 'domain name' in the glossary), the time and date you arrived, and what pages on the site interest you most.

Some people use their sites to go one stage further and try to gather more personal information about the people who visit them. One method is to use 'cookies'. The cookie is a file stored on the user's computer, often without their consent or knowledge. If you return to a site that has left a cookie on your computer, it can look at the cookie to find out what you did there before. For example, shopping sites remember what you bought and so gain an understanding of your personal preferences.

Other information can be gained without your knowledge as well, such as what programs you have on your computer and what other websites you've visited. It is even sometimes possible to get your email address.

Your privacy can be invaded even further when it comes to downloading files from the Internet. When you download a program file – something usually ending in .exe – then it is possible that absolutely everything on your computer could be accessed.

For many people this will come as quite a shock. While we are wary of joining mailing lists and giving out too much information over the Net, we may be less aware that information can already be taken from us without our knowledge.

 Top Tip: Help your children to get an understanding that there are often people behind websites who want to get information about them.

Hazard 3: Financial issues

When I was working for a charity a few years ago, I received an email from someone who said that they wanted to make a large donation to the organisation. They said that they wanted to move some money from Nigeria to the UK and needed a bit of help. In return, they promised to make a sizeable donation. Intrigued, if a little sceptical, I emailed back. I was then sent further details and a phone number to call. We had a chat on the phone, and he started to tell me how I could get hold of the money.

In the interim, however, I decided to do a search on the Internet using the keywords 'Nigeria' and 'hoax', and came up with a number of sites that explained what was going on. The email is a well-known fraud which appears under a number of different guises. The people perpetrating the scam try to gain your trust, tempt you with a large amount of money, and then get you to pay for the transfer of the money that they have promised you. However, once they've got hold of your money, they promptly disappear and you never hear from them again.

Children are more vulnerable to deception than we are, so they need to be made aware that there are people who will deliberately try to deceive them, although this is only a small minority of Net users.

One particularly big Internet industry that can be especially deceiving is gambling. Few gambling sites have clear warnings about under-age gambling, and about one fifth have no warnings at all,[22] so children won't automatically be warned away from them.

Some sites make offers that can be very attractive to children, such as promising to give them an amount of money as soon as they give them some credit card details and open an account with them. However, they will usually soon find that they have to use the account and gamble before they are allowed to get the money back.

In this matter, it's worth remembering that deception in financial matters can come from closer to home. While you need to keep your credit card details secure from people outside your family, it's probably worth keeping them out of temptation's way from your children too.

If your child has access to your credit card there is no reason why they can't use it online. It is theoretically possible that your children might purchase anything, from alcohol and pills to a new car or family holiday. The chances are that they won't consider that they are stealing from you, but do it with the best of intentions, thinking that they are making you money or snapping up a bargain!

 Top Tip: *Make it clear to your children that they are not to use your credit card online, and keep it out of sight to avoid temptation!*

Hazard 4: Cyberpests

There's been a great deal of publicity recently about stalkers, people who give unwanted and persistent attention. Although it doesn't happen all that often, it can be done online as easily as offline.

Online stalking or 'cyberstalking' is unwanted and unwelcome communication from someone through Internet venues of any type, including chatrooms, bulletin boards, email and discussion forums. At its most serious, stalkers may send threatening emails and viruses, and try to hack into computers. They may also send masses of unwelcome emails, some of them often sexually explicit. Some cyberstalkers post rude or obscene messages on discussion boards, or make unwelcome advances or false statements in chatrooms. They may even leave forged messages of all types, posing as you. This can also happen in guest books if you have a personal page or site.

Cyberstalking happens for many different reasons. Some cyberstalkers want to play out their fantasies online. It can begin in situations that seem completely harmless. It sometimes follows a meeting in chatrooms, or discussion on discussion boards. But the principle is the same. Somehow a cyberstalker has come across you, and they then decide to pursue you online.

Of course, it isn't just adults who can do it. Quite often it can be children having fun, unaware of the hurt and distress that they might be causing. But whoever does it, it is generally an unpleasant experience for the person being stalked.

Online bullying

One feature of cyberstalking can be online bullying. As many as one in four children in the UK have been the victims of online bullying in some shape or form. Around 7 per cent of children claim to have been harassed in Internet chatrooms, while 4 per cent say they've been bullied via email. Perhaps more upsetting, though, is that one third of children intimidated online hadn't told anyone about it.[23]

These figures show it's about as likely that your child will be bullied online at some time or another as they will be at school. So, as we've mentioned in earlier chapters, it's really vital that you foster a relationship with your children so that they feel able to come and talk to you about it if it does happen to them.

Cyberpredators

Although the danger from cyberstalkers and online bullies tends to be psychological, there are a very small number of people

123

who will go further. People with bad intentions may try to trick your children into meeting them face to face.

These people, often known as 'cyberpredators' will usually try to build a friendship with a child. They'll spend months trying to cultivate a relationship by email or in a chatroom. Children who seem lonely or unhappy may be particularly vulnerable. Cyberpredators may try to get hold of the child's address or telephone number and then call or send gifts. They may start sexual conversations. Often they'll pretend to be children themselves.

Children who meet in chatrooms and develop relationships will often try and meet the other person. As many as 86 per cent of one group of Internet users who use chatrooms, said that they had been asked for a face-to-face meeting with someone they met online.[24] Of course, the vast majority of these will be perfectly innocent. But when taken with the statistic that one third of teenage girls say they have been sexually harassed in a chatroom, it is a cause for concern.[25] Up to a quarter of young female Internet users say they've felt frightened or upset about things said to them during chatroom sessions. Girls are twice as likely as boys to have received unwanted comments of a sexual nature or repeated requests for face-to-face meetings.[26]

Top Tip: *If you are talking to your children about how to behave towards strangers when they are out of the house, why not talk about coming across strangers on the Internet at the same time?*

Warning signs

The last thing to say about watching out for the potential hazards and pitfalls on the Internet is that you can often tell all is not well by watching out for warning signs from your children.

Here are some warning signs to keep a special eye out for. If your children:

- are excessively secretive, hiding CDs or disks,
- use the computer late at night,
- quickly change the computer screen or program they are using when you are nearby,
- display sudden changes in their behaviour, e.g. inappropriate sexual knowledge, sleeping problems,

then you might want to keep a closer eye on them, and encourage them to talk a bit more about what they are doing online.

Remember, some of these things are also just natural behaviour for children, so don't panic!

 Top Tip: Don't be afraid of discussing what you might think is strange behaviour in your children with them. More often than not there is a perfectly good explanation!

Summary

- The vast majority of children have a very positive Internet experience and never encounter things that disturb them.
- The best way to make sure your children are safe is to be aware of what might happen and ensure that they are protected.
- There is a range of unsuitable material that, as a parent, you need to consider.
- There are a number of ways that children can come across inappropriate information by mistake, but they may also access it deliberately.
- While you are online it is possible for people to gain information about you without your knowledge, such as what programs you have on your computer and what other websites you've visited.
- Children are more vulnerable to deception than we are, so they need to be made aware that there are people who will deliberately try to mislead them.
- As parents, we should be aware that occasionally there are cyberstalkers or cyberpredators who might cause problems for our children.

THERE'S DANGEROUS MATERIAL OUT THERE ON THE NET...

OH NO! YOU MEAN OUR SCHOOL DINNER LADIES HAVE FINALLY LAUNCHED THEIR RECIPE WEBSITE?

Setting the boundaries

A middle-aged couple had been married for twenty-five years and were celebrating their wedding anniversary. During the party, a fairy appeared and said that because they had been such a loving couple all those years, she would give them one wish each.

The wife said, 'Now that the children have all left home, I would really like to travel all over the world.'

The fairy waved her wand and POOF! She had round-the-world tickets in her hand.

Next, it was the husband's turn. He paused for a moment, and then with a sly grin said, 'To be honest, after twenty-five years I am ready to move on. I'd like a wife twenty-five years younger than me.'

The fairy waved her wand and POOF! He was seventy.

There's an old saying that you should be careful what you wish for.

For those of us who wished we could give our children access to a learning tool that brought all the knowledge of the universe to the ends of our fingertips, at next to no cost – it came true with the Internet.

But, as we saw in the previous chapter, all resources – the print media, TV, radio or film – have the ability to educate and enhance our lives, but they also have the potential to do harm and damage.

Parents have always found ways of keeping their children safe from the risks that each of these resources bring, whether that meant calling for a rating system for films or ensuring that sexually explicit magazines are put on the top shelves in newsagents. Like most parents, you also probably have rules for how your children should deal with strangers, which TV programmes, films and videos they're allowed to watch, what shops they're allowed to enter, and where and how far from home they're allowed to travel. The Internet is similar. Once you're clued up and have rules you're happy with, there's no need to panic about it any more than you would worry about the TV programmes or films your children watch.

What you do and use to protect your children will depend on your own views of how you want to bring them up. It will also depend upon their ages, and how much you feel you can trust them. You will have to make difficult decisions, for example about whether you are going to let them surf unsupervised or use chatrooms. In this chapter we deal with some of the options available to you, and some of the issues that relate to each of those options.

But rather than approaching Internet safety as purely a problem, think of it as an opportunity. The lessons you and your children learn when grappling with dangers on the Net can apply to many other aspects of life. Knowing how to act carefully, avoiding dangerous places and thinking critically can serve your children well on dates, in the marketplace and in the voting booth as well as on the Internet.

> **Top Tip:** *A great place to learn about Internet safety and find useful information and resources is the Childnet International website at www. childnet-int.org.*

Dealing with inappropriate information – filtering software

One of the most talked-about things that parents can do to prevent their children accessing inappropriate information on the web is purchasing **filtering software** for their computer.

Filtering systems work in different ways, but are designed to look for keywords on web pages to identify the kind of content that they have. They sometimes also look at whether the computer or server that controls the site is known to host offensive material, and examine the domain name of a site. Others allow you to block specific sites that you don't want your family to be able to access, or work by having a huge directory of sites already established. If a website doesn't meet the standards you've decided on, the filtering system blocks access to it.

A lot of people don't realise it, but within both Microsoft's Internet Explorer and Netscape's Communicator browsers, there is also already a feature that allows you to select the kind of websites you would like your children to see.

All you have to do is set up your browser to indicate what kind of content you'll accept – for example, you can decide 'a little nudity, but no sex'. Every time someone then tries to access a website, the browser checks it first. If the site isn't up to scratch, the site is blocked.

Sounds good, doesn't it? In many ways it is. Filtering systems can sometimes work very effectively. But the most fundamental thing to grasp is that all filtering software, whether it's software that you buy or what's already on your computer, is limited.

I FOUND SOME FILTERING HARDWARE THAT WAS EVEN CHEAPER!

Part of the problem is that although filtering systems are getting more sophisticated, the vast amount of material on the web, and the speed with which it changes, puts limits on its abilities. It's simply impossible to make a program foolproof against all racist, pornographic and other harmful material.

These are some of the specific shortcomings of filtering software:

- It can exclude access to perfectly decent sites by identifying them wrongly.
- It can miss web pages that reveal their contents via graphics rather than text.
- Your children may feel that they are being limited.
- Children can sometimes get around the software.
- It tends only to look for English words and will let through offensive foreign-language sites.

The most effective programs are often those that only allow web users access to a pre-selected list of sites. But this, of course, blocks access to huge amounts of inoffensive, and potentially useful, information.

Programs that use several tactics to classify websites, such as looking for keywords on a site *and* the server that the page originally came from, tend to do a better job of preventing access to potentially offensive pages. Many will still classify some clearly offensive sites as safe, and exclude a lot of sites that are completely innocent. But they also usually need a lot of maintenance to keep their lists of safe sites up to date.

Clearly, filtering software can be a good idea but, given that it never works 100 per cent effectively, it should not be used in isolation to control how children use the web. There is no substitute for parental involvement.

Top Tip: One of the best ways to discover a good filtering program is to ask friends who have tried them.

TV or not TV?

One decision that parents have to make is whether their children should have Internet access – usually a computer – in their bedroom. It is a similar issue to whether your child is allowed a television.

But while a TV may show inappropriate material, it is usually after the 9 o'clock watershed. Some televisions also have the ability to block unsuitable channels. The Internet has no such watershed or so comprehensive a blocking mechanism, as we have seen. The dangers are all the more real because your child can interact online in a way that they can't with a television.

Keep the computer – and the TV for that matter – that your child uses in a shared family space wherever possible, particularly when your children are young. This provides accountability, but also means that you are more easily accessible to them should anything happen and they need your help.

Privacy

In the last chapter we highlighted how, as you move around the Internet, you leave 'cyber footprints', allowing people to gain information about you. However, it is possible to minimise how much information you give away by changing one or two basic settings on your computer, making it much harder for people to gain information about you and your children as they surf the Net.

One of the main ways is to set your computer so it can't accept cookies. If you are worried about cookies you can get your browser to refuse them. You can do this through your options on your Internet browser, which will probably have a privacy function where you can set a privacy level. For increased security or privacy you can also purchase security software on the Internet or at a computer shop.

By far the biggest threat to privacy, however, comes from filling in forms online, or giving out too much personal information in chatrooms or on discussion boards. We suggest that, as a general rule, you tell your children not to give out personal details without asking you first, at least until you feel that they are old enough to make these decisions for themselves.

This is something that children already seem to be grasping. Only one in ten of seven- to sixteen-year-olds polled in the UK in November 2001 would give out their home address online to get free samples, gifts or information.[27] However, this means that, although they are in the minority, too many children are still too free with personal information, so it's important to reiterate the need to be careful.

Dealing with unwanted email – protect your child from cyberstalkers

Every now and again, however, someone may get hold of your child's email address and you will receive unwanted email. Unwanted email can come in a variety of different forms – people bothering you deliberately, abusive mail, mail containing viruses, or people sending you junk mail that you haven't signed up for. Whatever the reason, if someone has got hold of your or your child's email address and you would rather they hadn't, there are ways of dealing with it.

If it's just that you've been added to a mailing list, there's usually information about how you can unsubscribe. If there isn't, then as a general rule it is best not to respond to unwanted email as it may encourage people to send you more.

The first thing to do is to keep a record of everything. Then you should find the account name of the person who is causing you trouble. The account name is not always the same as the screen name – the name you can see. Many ISPs will let you set a temporary screen 'alias' so that your real identity is hidden, but all ISPs have a method of checking the identity, profile or account information of someone who's in a chatroom or posting messages. You can contact your ISP for help discovering someone's identity, or look under 'Internet Header' in your email menu. You can then report the individual to their ISP, and in many cases ISPs will cancel the offender's account.

 Top Tip: You can look in the header for more information about who has sent unwanted emails.

Interacting with others on the Internet

Just as we tell our children to be wary of strangers they meet, we need to tell them to be wary of strangers on the Internet. Most people behave reasonably and decently online, but as we saw in the last chapter a few can also be potentially dangerous.

Teach your children that they should never:

- give out personal information (including their name, home address, phone number, age, race, family income, school name or location, or friends' names) or use a credit card online without your permission;
- share their password, even with friends;
- arrange a face-to-face meeting with someone they meet online unless you approve of the meeting and go with them to a public place;
- respond to messages that make them feel confused or uncomfortable; they should ignore the sender, end the communication, and tell you or another trusted adult right away;
- use bad language or send nasty messages online.

Learning about this can actually be fun for children. There are some sites that provide online games which they can play to teach them about Internet safety.

> ***Top Tip:*** *On the Childnet International website (www.childnet-int.org) there is an educational game where children can put two mystery people on the spot and ask them questions. Once they've heard all the answers, children pick their favourite and then see them close up.*

There are also some very positive things that your children can do themselves to increase their protection.

The first is to choose a nickname for use on discussion boards or chatrooms that doesn't reveal their gender or personal information. This can be a fun thing to do, as they can develop their own unique Internet identity.

Another is to teach your children to look closely at the sort of words and sentences people use when they write to them. Are they childlike? Are there double meanings in what they say? In this way they will learn to be careful, and it actually helps to develop skills in judging social situations that will be useful in other areas of life.

To snoop or not to snoop?

A decision that parents have to make is how much they are going to trust their children and how much they are going to check up on them.

You can find where your children have been on the Net by checking the history (or cache) in your browser. Both Microsoft's Internet Explorer and Netscape Navigator keep a history of sites visited. However, clever children who want to hide where they've been can clear that information, but many kids either don't know about that option or don't bother using it. For Internet Explorer 5.0, click on History on the tool bar. On the current version of Netscape, you can pull down the Communicator menu, select Tools and then select History.

The conclusions that you reach about this kind of thing will also probably influence whether you allow your child to password-protect areas of the computer.

DO YOU THINK YOU COULD MONITOR MY NET ACTIVITIES A LITTLE LESS CLOSELY?

Monitoring software

Monitoring or 'spy' software which tells you where your children are going on the Internet can, of course, be an alternative method for some parents to using filtering software. Monitoring software creates a log of where your kids have been or what they may have typed in email, chats, websites and newsgroups. Some software is so sophisticated, in fact, that even when you're not there you can record everything your children do on their PC and have a detailed report delivered to your email address – anywhere in the world – as frequently as every thirty minutes. You can specify the times and days of the week to record activity and send reports.

Once you have this information, you can then have a chat with your children about where they have been.

Top Tip: *Whether it's appropriate to monitor or block your children's access is a parental decision, but it's never a substitute for parenting.*

Search for your child's name

One good way of reassuring yourself about your child's welfare is to turn the potential dangers of the Internet into opportunities. While search engines can often bring up inappropriate information, it also means that you can check quite easily what is out there that might relate to your child.

Try searching for your child's name on AltaVista or other search engines that scour the entire Internet. Enter the full name in double quotes to avoid false results. It's not foolproof, but if your child (or anyone else) is posting his or her name on the Net, it might come up. You might also do the same thing with your child's email address. Consider doing similar searches with your family address, phone number and other personal information.

Draw up a contract

Some families have used a 'contract' that all the family members agree to abide by in an effort to promote positive, safe and responsible use of the Internet. The purpose of the contract is to make sure that children understand what's expected of them when using the Internet, so that there'll be no confusion about safe and responsible online use. But a family contract, if worded correctly, can also make responsibility a shared thing, and not another set of rules that children have to abide by. It also allows children to have a degree of control, in that they are accorded 'rights' as well.

A contract could go something like the one featured below, but you can add or take away things as you feel is right. It is a good idea to talk through the contract with your children, and allow them to have a say in what is in it.

Once you have agreed the content, the whole family can sign it. You might even decide to put it up next to the computer, as a reminder of what you have agreed.

The Contract

We realise that access to the Internet is a privilege, and that all members of our family should benefit from using it, whether it be in our education, work, hobbies, finances or relationships.

But we also recognise that all members of our family need to make safe and responsible choices while using

---

139

the Internet. We agree that we should all be able to feel safe, and that the consequences of not practising safe and responsible use of the Internet can be serious, dangerous and cause us trouble.

We therefore all agree to the following:

- Every family member should be able to explore, learn and enjoy information and activities on the Internet. Therefore every family member will be allowed regular time online.
- We will use the Internet only at the times agreed by the family, and perform only those things that we have decided are positive and of benefit.
- We will only visit websites that we all agree are appropriate to our various ages.
- While we are online, we will keep information about the family a secret. We will only give out personal information about ourselves online when the whole family agrees. This includes our real names, address, telephone number, name or location of our school or work, and names of our friends or relatives.
- We will not fill in online forms unless Mum or Dad has seen the form first.
- We will not upload or send pictures of ourselves, or any family member, to people that we don't know, without agreeing as a family that we should do so. When we send pictures to people we know, we will let the rest of the family know too.

- We will always show respect to other people we chat with on the Internet or by email, and have a right to expect the same from others.
- Every family member has a right not to be bothered or bullied by others, whether by people we know or people we don't know. If we think that we are being bullied, we will tell Mum or Dad.
- We understand that everything we see and everyone we meet online may not be telling the truth. We will always be careful to think about the information we receive while being online.
- We will not feel guilty if horrible pictures or words appear on our computer screen, on a website or in our emails. But we will tell Mum or Dad about anything that makes us feel uncomfortable.
- We can ignore emails and messages from people we don't know or trust and we will tell another family member if we think someone is acting weirdly or asking strange questions.
- We will not buy anything online without asking Mum or Dad first.
- The children in the family can discuss with Mum or Dad anything that they see or hear through the Internet. Children always have a right to ask for help from Mum, Dad or another trusted adult.
- Any family member has a right to ask another family member what they are doing online at any time, and we all commit to answering honestly.

> • We will never meet face to face or call on the telephone anyone we have met online without first telling other family members, including Mum or Dad, that we are doing so.

You will no doubt have things that you want to add or take away from the example above. But we suggest that it is a very good idea to commit things to paper in this way. In so doing, boundaries and expectations are made clear, and you can be sure that you have communicated the important things to your children.

HAS THE 'FAMILY NET CONTRACT' STOPPED YOUR KIDS VIEWING INAPPROPRIATE SITES?

YES - I TAPED IT IN FRONT OF THE SCREEN.

Summary

- Filtering systems work in different ways, and although they can be effective, they are all limited.
- You can guard your privacy by changing the settings on your computer or buying additional software.
- It is good to consider keeping the computer that your child uses in a shared family space.
- If you receive nuisance email, keep a record of it.
- A parent will need to decide how closely they want to monitor their child's Internet activity.

WHY SPEND TIME
SURFING WHEN
YOU CAN
DIVE
RIGHT IN!

"RESOURCES"

It's a wonderful World Wide Web

The Internet can sometimes seem quite overwhelming with the sheer volume of sites that you can visit. And there is no guarantee that, among the millions, you will be able to find what you are looking for. Indeed, you can often spend hours trying to track down information that you need, only to end up abandoning your quest, defeated and frustrated.

There are certain websites, however, that will be a great help to you and your family in your everyday life – if you can find them.

Over the last few years we have come across some sites that we have used regularly and have found an invaluable source of information and help. We have whittled them down to the few which we have listed below, with a bit of information about what you might find when you visit.

In choosing them we have gone for the more established sites that we are pretty sure won't suddenly disappear! But it should be borne in mind that this is just to get you thinking – there are dozens that we could have included. The various government departments, such as the Treasury or the Department for Education and Skills, for example, have some very useful information if you are doing a tax return or want to know about schools.

Below, there should be something for every member of the family!

BBC
http://www.bbc.co.uk

The BBC is one of the most popular sites for European surfers, and you will see why as soon as you arrive. The quantity of information is quite simply vast, and there seems to be at least one thing there for everyone.

If you want news coverage this is the place to go. Including the latest headlines, commentary and features on what is going on in the world, you can read the text and receive audio and video reports. Coming from the BBC, it is all of a very high standard, and you can also sometimes see things that aren't being broadcast on TV or radio, or catch up with things you might have missed.

Another thing that appeals about this site is the fantastic children's section, with many things to do online. It ties in very well with Children's BBC, with games, information and things to do with children connected to their favourite children's TV characters. This is at http://www.bbc.co.uk/cbbc/.

If you want to introduce a very young child to the Internet, this is one of the sites that we would start with, as there are some very simple games where you colour in pictures and then print them off, which children as young as three can do.

There is material for older children, too. There are often webcasts and chat sessions by people who have just been on TV, meaning that you can go to the site and ask them questions. If you are a sports fan, you can also get the latest news and results.

 Top Tip: Why not visit the BBC site with your child and take part in an online chat with one of the characters from their favourite TV programme?

TheAA.com
http://www.theaa.com

It might be a bit of a shock, but the AA website isn't just worth a visit if you are a driving enthusiast!

Although it's a bit bland in its presentation, don't be put off by its style. The site is highly functional and extremely useful for most things to do with travel and planning a journey – particularly if you are going by car.

The site has all the usual stuff you would expect, covering breakdown cover, finances and insurance, but it also contains some surprising features such as ideas for keeping the children happy during holidays, and places to go.

During the holiday time, this site comes into its own both for children and for adults. There are guides to restaurants and pubs, hotels and weekend breaks. But perhaps the most useful facility is the 'routefinder'. Just type in where you are leaving from and where you are going to, and the AA gives you detailed directions and estimated travelling times. It will also give you information on the traffic blackspots to avoid.

If you are planning a holiday, there is also a worldwide search facility that compares extremely favourably with other sites that offer holiday deals. One particularly appealing feature is that it allows you to search specifically for family-friendly holidays, which many other travel sites don't have.

> **Top Tip:** Why not introduce your child to budgeting and include them in the journey planning by doing a search on the site before a car journey to find the cheapest petrol stations?

NHS Direct
http://www.nhsdirect.nhs.uk/

Not a particularly fun site, and not for the hypochondriacs, but NHS Direct has probably everything you will want in terms of information about health for your family.

The site aims to put a variety of reliable health information resources at your fingertips, helping you to make informed choices about your health and lifestyle.

The features include an online encyclopedia with a comprehensive guide to hundreds of common medical conditions.

There are sections on diagnosis and treatments along with explanatory diagrams and images. There is also a self-help guide containing advice on what to do next for a range of common symptoms, plus background information on minor ailments and guidance on what you should have in your medicine cabinet. There is also a good collection of information in audio format, and you can sift through a selection of the College of Health's audio files.

If you are thinking about a bit of a change in lifestyle, there is a 'Healthy Living' section which includes tips on what you should and shouldn't be doing, plus a separate section on reducing the risks of major diseases.

It also includes a link to another very helpful resource in the form of a search engine which allows you to track down full details of GPs, pharmacies (chemists) and dentists in your area. This is extremely useful if you are new to the area in which you live.

Should you find that the site doesn't answer your questions, there are a couple of other options too. The first is a health enquiry facility. You complete an online form and it automatically sends your question to a nurse who will reply. It may be a bit of a wait, but they promise to give you an individual response in five days.

The second option is what they call a 'health information gateway'. This is a directory of links to selected websites and other resources for a range of medical conditions.

Top Tip: *If your child gets ill with a minor ailment or gets hurt with a cut or scrape, why not use it as an educational experience and visit the site to learn more about it?*

Educate the Children
http://www.educate.org.uk

We think that Educate the Children is probably the best education site in the UK.

The site is divided into various zones, including: a parent zone with guidelines to understanding the education system and how it affects your child, and tips on how you can get involved in your child's education and school; a teacher zone with thousands of lesson plans, worksheets, articles and teaching strategies available to view and download; and a learning zone with puzzles, colouring sheets, fact files and SATs revision help.

It doesn't just focus on school, however. One feature of the site is 'Out and About', a database of child-friendly places and activities throughout the UK.

Although this site is geared more towards primary children, it incorporates quite a few elements from schoolsnet.com, which isn't. Schoolsnet was launched in November 1999 to offer parents, pupils and teachers an indispensable educational resource. This has things that parents will find particularly useful, including:

- a schools guide for every school and university in the UK, with information including examination results, inspection reports and detailed background;
- a library of over 2,000 titles;
- a reference area for education professionals;
- a shop;
- education news;
- classroom resources for both parents and teachers;
- a great range of links.

Top Tip: *If you have had a successful trip or activity somewhere with your child, why not help them by submitting it for inclusion in their online database, so others can experience it too?*

Ask Jeeves for Kids
http://www.ajkids.com/

For those not familiar with the Ask Jeeves concept, Ask Jeeves is a search engine that is slightly different from most other search engines in that you type in questions rather than key-words.

Ask Jeeves for Kids is the children's version, and a very easy way for children to find answers to questions. The advantage is that it gives the user help in finding what they are looking for. Ask Jeeves allows you to ask a question in plain English and, after interacting with you to confirm the question, the search

151

engine takes you to one, and only one, website that answers your question.

Of course, it doesn't work every time and needs to be used in conjunction with other search engines, but the advantage is that it uses sophisticated natural language processing to understand and direct questions to an extensive knowledge base.

The search engine has its own resource that consists of thousands of question templates and millions of researched 'answer links' to websites. It works because the research staff that run the site select questions and then search the Internet for the best sites that answer the questions. The Ask Jeeves knowledge base is built by humans, not by software 'spiders', and therefore each answer link should be relevant to the question asked. This saves users countless hours of searching on their own, and helps to avoid the frustrations that many children can experience when searching for what they want.

> **Top Tip:** *If your children ask you a general knowledge question, why not sit down with them and find the answer together on Ask Jeeves for Kids?*

Yahoo.com
http://www.yahoo.co.uk

Yahoo is probably best known as a search engine but it is also a huge web portal (or 'way in' to the Internet).

If it is information that you want, Yahoo is a portal with an absolutely massive range of content. If you are searching the Internet for anything, Yahoo should probably be one of your first ports of call.

Yahoo is also the kind of site that you might want to set up as your home page. One of the great features is that even though there is a great deal of content, you can customise what you see on the site to your own needs when you visit.

By registering with Yahoo you get a log-in ID and then select the kind of content that you would like it to display every time that you return. You can get a Yahoo email account, and your own online address book and calendar that will automatically send you reminders about appointments, birthdays and other important dates.

Yahoo has lots of partnerships with other websites and content providers, which means that you get some of the best stuff on the web all under one heading, including lots of search facilities. So whether you want to shop, look up holiday deals, get the weather forecast or stock market quotes, or buy a house, there are lots of databases to search right there on the site.

There is quite a bit for both young and older children too. You can watch pop videos on the music channel, as well as downloading games or playing them right there online. You can find out the weather and temperature anywhere in the world, and there is a massive finance channel and shopping channel too.

The only drawback is that there is lots of content that you might easily miss! It is therefore worth spending a while looking around. After all, you don't always know what you want until you find it!

> **Top Tip:** You can use Yahoo to send a whole range of email greeting cards for birthdays, anniversaries or special days, and they are all free!

Alfy.com
http://www.alfy.com

ALFY is the largest web portal for children, and was developed so that three- to nine-year-olds could safely and easily experience everything the cyber world has to offer. ALFY is a fun, accessible but also educational centre stocked with interactive stories, games, crafts, activities, and much more.

Designed with the guidance of an advisory board of world-leading psychologists and educators, ALFY is revolutionising the way kids learn and play online.

One reassuring feature is that the site is particularly concerned with children's safety issues. All sites that it links to are hand-selected by a team of educators to ensure that they are in compliance with their child safety guidelines. In addition, ALFY offers 'ALFY shield', a unique filtering software that parents and teachers can download free to protect their children from coming into contact with inappropriate content. This program restricts children from entering any sites outside ALFY, so preventing them from encountering any offensive material, and is ideal for younger children.

The site has also been very well thought out. It is particularly attractive to younger children because there are lots of sounds, as characters talk to you. ALFY's presentation is also entirely graphical. The colourful animated graphics, combined with the sounds, make the site easy for young kids to navigate.

An educational dimension with opportunities to develop literacy, numeracy and reasoning skills also adds to the value of the site significantly. Kids can even play different musical instruments, record their melodies and listen to their creations. The site offers hundreds of engaging activities designed to stimulate young children, and because of the safety features you can feel happy to leave them there on their own.

Top Tip: *For younger children, when you think that they are ready, why not let them use the Internet for the first time through ALFY?*

Handbag.com
http://www.handbag.com

Handbag.com was launched in October 1999 and is a fifty/fifty joint venture between Boots and a media company. It was the first women's website to launch in the UK and is currently generally considered to be the leading site for women.

Handbag.com aims to provide the inside track for busy women online, on everyday important issues like relationships, health, careers and beauty. The site includes expert advice, discussion groups and email, plus tips and articles on everything from fashion to parenting. It has a good quality of writing as it draws experts and a breadth of coverage; these have established its reputation as the leader in a crowded field.

The site is aimed at women between twenty-five and forty-five who enjoy going to the cinema and reading magazines – particularly the women's and home improvements titles. It's full of tips and advice about health and beauty, fashion, money and shopping, quizzes, online voting, etc.

The only thing to be cautious about is that this isn't really a site for children. Some of the content is similar to women's magazines and so deals with some adult themes.

 Top Tip: *Handbag.com can be a great place to retreat to for mothers who have a few minutes to relax.*

uSwitch.com
http://www.uswitch.com

This is a classic site in terms of showing how the Internet can save you significant money.

uSwitch.com is a free, impartial comparison service which helps customers compare online the prices on gas, electricity, home telephone and digital television. All you do is enter the details of who you are, where you live and how much electricity, gas or other service you use and they do the rest, right there on the site, in a matter of seconds.

Set up in February 2000, the site aims to help customers take advantage of the best prices, offers and services from every supplier. The endeavour is to make it as easy as possible to compare and switch providers.

uSwitch.com is independent of all the companies it represents. Unlike traditional brokers who work on commission, they show you all gas, electricity and digital television suppliers, and a whole range of home telephone providers – not just the ones that pay them a commission.

We used the site and switched our electric and gas suppliers, and found that it saved us several hundred pounds a year. The service is based on the most up-to-date information from suppliers and regulators so you can be assured that the calculations are accurate.

The company behind the website is owned by private investors. None of the suppliers they represent have a stake in the company, which is also reassuring.

The uSwitch.com website ranks number 2 in the UK for utilities sector. It receives more visitors than all of the supplier sites except British Gas. It also has plans to add other features, which are likely to be just as useful if what they have got already is anything to go by.

Top Tip: *Why not use uSwitch.com as part of a review of your family finances? You can even involve your children or entice them to help you with the promise of a share in any savings that you make!*

Science
http://www.nhm.ac.uk
http://www.HowStuffWorks.com

We have cheated a bit here, and included two sites which we recommend visiting. The first is www.nhm.ac.uk – the Natural History Museum. Not only is this educational but it's a site to have a whole load of fun with, too. The great feature is their interactive section with great use of sound and pictures. The section includes an ant cam with live pictures of the museum's leafcutter ant colony, a dino directory with a click-down map, and a game that lets you mix together animal and environmental sounds from around the world to make your own piece of rhythmic music; these are just some of the interactive features that they have that makes natural history on the web fun!

The other site we recommend is www.HowStuffWorks.com. This is one of the most visited sites on the web, and is great for the inquisitive mind. Millions of people have described HowStuffWorks content as reliable, accurate and entertaining. Originally founded as a website for curious people, the award-winning company now offers clear and fascinating content through various media channels to millions of readers every month. Recognised internationally as the leading provider of information on how things work, HowStuffWorks explains the world from the inside out!

Glossary

Access – usually a term referring to the process of logging on to the Internet. The idea of 'access' comes from the notion that you are accessing a computer system and establishing a connection to other computers.

Account name – when you sign up with an Internet Service Provider (ISP) you are given an 'account'. That account will have a name (or 'username') and a password allowing you to access the Internet through them.

Address – a series of letters, numbers and/or symbols by which you are identified on the Internet and by which you identify yourself. You can, for example, have a web address, which is where people can find your website, or an email address where people can send you email.

Attachment – a file (or group of files) included (or 'attached') with an email message.

Bandwidth – the amount of information that can flow through a channel, expressed in cycles per second (hertz). It also refers to the range of frequencies (not the speed) or the measured amount of information that can be transmitted over a connection: the higher the frequency, the higher the bandwidth and the greater the capacity to carry information.

Blind copy (bcc) – an option in an email program that allows you to send the same message to many different addresses without anyone else knowing. You put a recipient's e-mail address in the 'bcc' field, meaning that the recipients cannot see each other's email addresses and so don't know that someone else received it.

Bookmark – both a verb and a noun, it is to mark a web page as a 'favourite', which stores it in a list on your browser (each item on the list is called a bookmark). This allows you to re-access the page by clicking on the bookmark, rather than typing the address again.

Broadband – a high-speed method of data transmission that sends and receives information on coaxial cable or fibre-optic, which is faster than conventional telephone lines. This means that you can, for example, make phone calls and carry video and other data all at the same time.

Browser – a program such as Microsoft Internet Explorer or Netscape Navigator which is used by your computer to view web pages.

Bulletin board or *bulletin board system (BBS)* – a meeting and announcement system for obtaining online information and services, including carrying on discussions, uploading and downloading files.

Cache – both a verb and a noun, it is either the action of storing web files for later re-use or the term used to describe where those files are stored. It is a form of memory. When you're on the web, web pages, graphics and multimedia elements are stored or 'cached' on your computer so that when you return to that particular web page the information doesn't have to be downloaded all over again. This makes browsing the Internet faster.

Carbon copy (cc) – like the 'bcc' function it is an option in email programs that allows you to send duplicate copies of an email message. But, unlike the 'bcc' function, when you type a recipient's email address into the 'cc' field it is viewable to everyone who receives the email message.

Channel – the term for an area on a website that contains information on a specific topic or subject, in a similar way to a specialised TV or radio channel.

Chatroom – a website or area of a website used for live online conversation where a number of people can type messages to each other. These messages usually appear on an area of the screen next to the user's nickname, 'screen name' or 'handle'. Many chatrooms have a particular topic which you are expected to discuss; others are purely for meeting other people.

Click – the action of pressing and releasing the mouse button, usually to select or activate something on your computer.

Content – the name for the creative contribution of the writers, artists, animators and musicians whose work makes up the text, artwork, animation and music on the Net.

Cookie – a small piece of information about you or your computer that is sent to your PC when you browse certain websites.

Cyberpredators – people with bad intent who may try to trick you or your children into meeting them, through online contact.

Cyberspace – the name used to describe the digital world, and in particular the Internet. Perceived as an 'immaterial realm of data' or some kind of virtual world, it is, of course, actually a physical infrastructure. The term was coined by William Gibson in his novel *Neuromancer.*

Cyberstalking – the uninvited and unwelcome communication from another through Internet venues of any type, including chatrooms, bulletin boards, email, discussion forums.

Database driven – a term usually used to describe a website that organises a vast amount of data and allows it to be retrieved on demand.

Dial-up connection – one of the cheapest and most popular ways for someone to access the Internet, using standard telephone lines and a modem.

Directory – best thought of as the 'table of contents' found on a web server, a computer disk or a computer. A directory, sometimes called a folder, often lists names of files, their size, when they were created, and what kind of files they are.

Discussion board – a place on the web where people can post and read written discussions on topics of common interest. A person submits or posts a message on the board either by sending an email or by filling in a form on a website.

Domain name – a user-friendly way of expressing the address of a website. Addresses are usually expressed in numbers (the IP address) but domain names are in word form so that they can be more easily found. Domain names usually begin with www. and are typed into web browsers to bring up the website.

Download – to transfer a file or files from one computer to another. When you access a web page, you are essentially 'downloading' the page from the server on which it is hosted. But you can also download specific files from some websites in order to gain access to data such as music, film, radio and text documents.

E-card – an electronic version of a greeting card, sent to an email address, usually from a website.

Email – mail that's electronically transmitted by your computer instantaneously, anywhere in the world.

163

Emoticon – a sequence of typed characters that creates a rough picture of something such as a facial expression, which is usually used to convey an emotion. Also known as a smiley.

Filtering software – a program that examines incoming data to ensure that only information within certain parameters is allowed to pass through.

Flaming – a slanging match between two or more people, usually by email or in chatrooms.

Hardware – the electronic components and computer equipment that make up a computer system.

Information superhighway – another term for the Internet.

Internet – a vast network of networks.

Internet Service Provider (ISP) – a company that provides people with access to the Internet, and often web space and an email address too.

Keyword – a word that you type into a search engine in order to begin an online search.

Local Area Network (LAN) – a network that connects computers in a relatively small area such as a room, a building or a set of buildings.

Mailbox – the place where your email messages are stored. This will either be on your computer, if you use an email program, or on the server of your email provider if you check your email online.

Modem – a device you connect to your computer or inside your computer which then connects to a phone line. It enables the computer to talk to other computers through the phone system. In a nutshell, modems do for computers what a telephone does for humans.

Mouse – a piece of equipment connected to your computer and used to position the cursor or pointer on your screen.

Net radio – a form of broadcasting radio over the Internet.

Network – a collection of two or more computers that are linked together with communications equipment. Once connected, each part of the network can share the software, hardware and information contained in the other parts.

Online – the state of being connected to the Internet.

Operating system – the foundation software of a computer system.

Password – a combination of letters and other symbols needed to log into a computer, a computer system or program. Things are password protected when they require a password to access them.

Personal computer – a computer designed for use by one person at a time.

Screen name – an Internet alias that can be used in such places as chatrooms and discussion boards.

Search engine – a website with a program that acts as a catalogue for the Internet. Search engines attempt to index and locate desired information by searching for the keywords that someone specifies.

Server – a server is usually a big computer that provides the information, files, web pages and other services such as email. The word 'server' is also used to describe the software and operating system designed to run server hardware. An analogy is often drawn to a restaurant with waiters and customers. You, the customer, order a file or a web page, and the server gives them to you.

Smiley – see 'emoticon'.

Software – a set of instructions that tells a computer how to execute functions and tasks.

Spam – an email message sent to someone without their consent. This is usually done on a large scale with thousands of people receiving the same unsolicited message. The term comes from Monty Python. Also known as 'junk mail'.

Surf – to browse or look up information on the web.

Unsubscribe – to remove your name and email address from a mailing list or discussion group. This is usually done by sending an email.

Username – the name you use to identify yourself when you access certain programs, websites or networks.

WAP or Wireless Application Protocol – a specific technology developed for wireless devices such as mobile phones, designed to enable access to the Internet and special services.

Web – short name for the World Wide Web.

Web ring – a chain of websites that have chosen to link to each other, usually because they have a common theme. Visitors to a site in a web ring are invited to visit the next site in the chain, and so on until they arrive back where they started.

Wide Area Network (WAN) – a network that uses high-speed, long-distance communications to connect computers over large distances.

Notes

1 A new report from Continental Research (16 August 2002) has found that there are now 17.9 million adults in the UK who use the Internet on a regular basis from home and/or work.
2 According to a survey published in August 2001 by NOP Family, a division of NOP World, three-quarters of British children aged between seven and sixteen now have Internet access. In the six months to April 2001, the number of Internet users in this age group grew by 10 per cent to 5.6 million.
3 Nine in ten of these users aged between seven and sixteen say in the survey by the NOP Research Group that the Internet helps them with their learning.
4 PC Advisor (www.pcadvisor.co.uk) reports that a large number of UK parents feel the Internet is just as important as traditional resources for their child's learning. According to a study conducted by BT Openworld, 48 per cent of parents with school-going children said that the Internet was as good as other media. Around 45 per cent of UK parents believe that the Internet is a better learning tool than television.
5 Source: Markle Foundation, July 2001: 'Toward a Framework for Internet Accountability'.
6 Royal Bank of Scotland survey. Taylor Nelson Sofres questioned 1,000 people by telephone between 30 April and 2 May 2002.

7 The study was initially based on a random telephone survey with 3,533 people in March 2000. The new findings are based on 1,501 follow-up interviews conducted a year later.

8 A Nielsen NetRatings study.

9 Continental Research, August 2002.

10 Virginstudent, 13 July 2001: only 1 per cent of UK college and university students have never used the Internet. The study, from Virginstudent. com, found that a third of students use the Internet every day, while over half use it three to five times a week. Two-thirds of students own their own computer, and 58 per cent of first-year students brought their own computer to college with them. Email is the most popular use of the Internet by students, followed by study, entertainment, sports info, news and travel.

11 Silicon.com: the Net is the third source of news for UK users, 29 July 2002. People in the UK spend three times longer surfing the Internet than they do reading newspapers, reports Silicon.com. This is according to a new survey commissioned by the British ISP, Freeserve.The study found that those aged between sixteen and thirty-four spend fifteen times longer on the Net in an average week than they do reading a newspaper. The Internet is now established as the third source of news for British citizens, behind television and radio. Newspapers and magazines have moved down to fourth and fifth place respectively.

12 According to a survey published in March 2001 by the NOP Research Group.

13 The Internet User Profile Survey.

14 Continental Research, August 2002.

15 The Royal Bank of Scotland survey. Taylor Nelson Sofres questioned 1,000 people by telephone between 30 April and 2 May 2002.

16 Taylor Nelson Sofres survey for Royal Bank of Scotland. Just 43 per cent of women made purchases over the Internet compared to 54 per cent of men.

17 Continental Research, August 2002.

18 NFO WorldGroup, 'Kids join in online shopping process', 14 August 2001: 74 per cent of US parents who shop online allow their children to take part in the online buying process. The NFO WorldGroup says that 72 per cent of children are allowed to pick the colours of goods purchased

online. Children take charge of pointing and clicking 48 per cent of the time, and suggest websites to buy from 42 per cent of the time. Forty per cent of online shopping families said they planned to spend more online in the next three months than they did in the same period last year.

19 NOP Research Group, 30 July 2001: a survey by NOP found that one in ten of the young people polled said they had seen something on the Internet that upset or embarrassed them.

20 NCTE, 18 July 2002: the preliminary findings of an EU study on Internet safety in Ireland, Belgium, the UK and Greece suggest that 24 per cent of children between the ages of eight and seventeen have accidentally encountered pornography while online.

21 MessageLabs, 29 July 2002: nearly 15 per cent of emails received each day by British firms contain Spam, according to a new survey from the email security company MessageLabs.

22 Federal Trade Commission, 27 June 2002: the Federal Trade Commission found that many child-orientated online game sites carried ads for age-restricted gambling websites. The Commission also visited over a hundred popular gambling websites and found that it was easy for minors to access the sites because there are few effective blocking mechanisms.

23 NCH, 'A quarter of UK kids have been bullied online', 15 April 2002: one in four children in the UK have been the victims of online bullying, according to a new study from the children's charity, NCH. Over 16 per cent of young people said they had received bullying or threatening text messages sent via mobile phones. Around 7 per cent claimed to have been harassed in Internet chatrooms, while 4 per cent had been bullied via email. NCH reveals that 29 per cent of children intimidated online hadn't told anyone about it.

24 NCTE, 18 July 2002: the preliminary findings of an EU study on Internet safety in Ireland, Belgium, the UK and Greece suggest that as many as 86 per cent of young Irish Internet users who use chatrooms say that they have been asked for a face-to-face meeting with someone they met online.

25 Girl Scout Research Institute, 11 March 2002: 30 per cent of teenage girls polled by the Girl Scout Research Institute said they had been sexually harassed in a chatroom. Only 7 per cent, however, had told

their mothers or fathers about the harassment, as they were worried that their parents would ban them from going online. Most of the girls surveyed said they tried to avoid pornographic sites, but said they frequently received pornographic Spam, or accidentally ended up on a porn site. When the respondents were asked how they knew what was safe online behaviour, 84 per cent said they followed their own common sense. Fifty-one per cent said they learned from their parents, and 4 per cent said, 'Nothing is that bad online because it's not really real.' The GSRI said parents should pay attention to their daughters' online activities. Eighty-six per cent of the girls polled said they could chat online without their parents' knowledge, 57 per cent could read their parents' email, and 54 per cent could conduct a cyber relationship.

26 Ipsos-Reid, 2 February 2001: up to a quarter of young female Internet users say they have felt frightened or upset about things said to them during chatroom sessions. Girls were twice as likely as boys to have received unwanted comments of a sexual nature or repeated requests for face-to-face meetings. The report, which includes survey results from sixteen countries, found that in some countries, such as Mexico, Germany, Canada and the US, almost half of young chatroom participants have gone on to have ongoing email exchanges with people they first met in chatrooms. Most teenagers and young adults, however, are unlikely to arrange a face-to-face meeting with someone they met online.

27 NOP Research Group, 18 January 2002: a report from NOP indicates that children who use the Internet are wising up to online dangers. Only 11 per cent of seven- to sixteen-year-olds polled in the UK the previous November would give out their home address online to get free samples, gifts or information. In June 2000, 29 per cent would have done so. Of those who would not give their home address online, 41 per cent said it was because their parents had told them not to, up from 33 per cent in the previous year.

Further information

Parentalk
PO Box 23142
London SE1 0ZT

Tel: 020 7450 9073
Fax: 020 7450 9060
email: info@parentalk.co.uk

Website: www.parentalk.co.uk

*Provides a range of resources and
services designed to inspire parents
to make the most of every stage of
their child's growing (see back pages
of this book).*

**Internet safety and education organisations
and other useful websites**

Childnet International
Studio 14
Brockley Cross Business Centre
96 Endwell Road
London SE4 2PD

Tel: 020 7639 6967
Fax: 020 7639 7027
email: info@childnet-int.org

Website: www.childnet-int.org

*Childnet International is a charity
committed to making the Internet a
great and safe place for children.*

Resources include:

www.kidsmart.co.uk – *a practical Internet safety resource for primary schools, which contains helpful tips for parents.*

www.launchsite.org – *activities and resources for parents.*

Safekids

Website: www.safekids.com
Website: www.safekids.com/
  safeteens

These sites contain tips and suggestions to make your family's online experience fun and productive.

BBC

Website: www.bbc.co.uk
Website: www.bbc.co.uk/webwise

Safety tips and guide to the Internet.

For Kids By Kids Online

(FKBKO)
Cyberspace Research Unit
Chandler Building
University of Central Lancs
Preston
Lancs PR1 2HE

Tel: 01772 893755/6
email: ro-connell@uclan.ac.uk

Website: www.fkbko.net

A great interactive entertaining site for kids by kids about Internet safety, with ideas for sites to visit.

Internet Content Rating

22 Old Steine
Brighton
East Sussex BN1 1EL

Tel: 01273 648332
Fax: 01273 648331

Website: www.icra.org

Empowers parents to make informed decisions about electronic media by labelling the content. Aims to protect children from potentially harmful material.

Internet Watch Foundation

5 Coles Lane
Oakington
Cambridgeshire CB4 5BA

Tel: 01223 237700
Fax: 01223 235921

Website: www.iwf.org.uk

Works to educate and raise awareness of issues surrounding the Internet, promoting the use of filtering systems and rating of Internet content. Runs an online hotline form where users can report material they believe to be illegal. Please note that offensive material cannot be reported over the phone.

Quick
Website: www.quick.org.uk

Helps children with online research.

Government departments/agencies

British Educational Communications and Technology Agency
Millburn Hill Road
Science Park
Coventry CV4 7JJ

Tel: 024 7641 6994
Fax: 024 7641 1418
email: becta@becta.org.uk

Website: www.becta.org.uk

Becta is the government's lead agency for ICT in education. It supports the UK government and national organisations in the use and development of ICT in education to raise standards, widen access, improve skills and encourage effective management.

The Home Office
Customer Information Service
7th floor
50 Queen Anne's Gate
London SW1H 9AT

Tel: 0870 0001585 (9 a.m.–5 p.m.) for general enquiries

Textphone: 020 7273 3476 (9 a.m.–5 p.m.) phone for the hard of hearing
Fax: 020 7273 2065
email: public.enquiries@home office.gsi.gov.uk

Produces websites and information on Internet safety issues:

www.thinkuknow.co.uk – *a site for children on how to stay safe using chatrooms.*

www.wiseuptothenet.co.uk – *gives help and advice on keeping your child safe on the Internet.*

The Department for Education and Skills (DfES)
Great Smith Street
London SW1P 3BT

Tel: 0870 000 2288
Fax: 01928 79 4248
email: info@dfes.gsi.gov.uk

Websites: www.dfes.gov.uk
www.parentsonline.gov.uk

The DfES website has excellent links for parents, teachers and children and a wealth of information on school life and how parents can help children with key skills. Parents Online has been set up to help parents understand the educational benefits of the Internet.

DfES Parents' Gateway

Website: www.dfes.gov.uk/parents

Contains direct links to the Parents' Centre and other related websites.

In Scotland

The Scottish Executive Education Department
1B Victoria Quay
Edinburgh EH6 6QQ

Tel: 0131 244 0911
Enquiry line: 08457 741741
email: ceu@scotland.gov.uk

Website: www.scotland.gov.uk

The first port of call for further information on education in Scotland.

In Wales

The Education Department
National Assembly for Wales,
Crown Building
Cathays Park
Cardiff CF10 3NQ

Tel: 029 2082 5111

Website: www.wales.gov.uk

For details of local variations of provision and curriculum for Wales, e.g. Welsh language teaching.

In Northern Ireland

Department of Education
Rathgael House
43 Balloo Rd
Bangor
County Down BT19 7PR

Tel: 028 9127 9279
Fax: 028 9127 9100
email: mail@deni.gov.uk

Website: www.deni.gov.uk

Useful organisations and websites (general)

BBC Parenting Website

Website: www.bbc.co.uk/health/parenting

Childalert

email: info@childalert.co.uk

Website: www.childalert.co.uk

Childalert is an information service for parents and anyone else looking after children. It provides information about child safety and well-being in the home and on the move, covering pre-conception to the first weeks at home, to the energy and determination of toddlers, to the concerns of raising boys and girls and how different they can be.

Childcare Link
Website: www.childcarelink.gov.uk

Information for parents about childcare in England and Scotland.

Citizens Advice Bureau (CAB)
Website: www.nacab.org.uk

A free and confidential service giving information and advice on topics such as: benefits; maternity rights; debts; housing, consumer, employment and legal problems; family and personal difficulties. It also has details of useful national and local organisations. Ask at your local library or look in your phone book for your nearest office. Opening times may vary.

Education Extra
17 Old Ford Rd
London E2 9PL

Tel: 020 8709 9900
Fax: 020 8709 9933
email: info@educationextra.org.uk

Website: www.educationextra.org.uk

Supports out-of-school-hours learning.

Home-Start UK
2 Salisbury Road
Leicester LE1 7QR

Tel: 0116 233 9955
Fax: 0116 233 0232
email: info@home-start.org.uk

Website: www.home-start.org.uk

In Northern Ireland
Home-Start
133 Bloomfield Avenue
Belfast BT5 5AB

Tel/Fax: 028 9046 0772
email: heather.knox@homestartni.co.uk

Volunteers offer support, friendship and practical help to young families in their own homes.

Kids Club Network
Bellerive House
3 Muirfield Crescent
London E14 9SZ

Tel: 020 7512 2100

Website: www.kidsclubs.com

Offers information and advice on school-aged childcare.

National Children's Bureau
8 Wakley Street
London WC1V 7QE

Tel: 020 7843 6000
Fax: 020 7278 9512
email: membership@ncb.org.uk

Website: www.ncb.org.uk

The National Children's Bureau (NCB) promotes the interests and well-being of all children and young people across every aspect of their lives. It advocates the participation of children and young people in all matters affecting them.

National Family and Parenting Institute

430 Highgate Studios
53–79 Highgate Road
London NW5 1TL

Tel: 020 7424 3460
Fax: 020 7485 3590
email: info@nfpi.org

Website: www.nfpi.org

An independent charity set up to provide a strong national focus on parenting and families in the twenty-first century.

NHS Direct

Twenty-four-hour advice line: 0845 4647

Website: www.nhsdirect.co.uk

NHS Direct Online is a website providing high-quality health information and advice for the people of Britain. It is unique in being supported by a twenty-four-hour nurse advice and information helpline.

NSPCC (National Society for the Prevention of Cruelty to Children)

Weston House
42 Curtain Road
London EC2A 3NH

Helpline: 0800 800 5000
Tel: 020 7825 2500
Fax: 020 7825 2525

Website: www.nspcc.org.uk

Internet issues link: www.nspcc.org.
   uk/html/home/needadvice/
   helpyourchildsurfinsafety.htm

Aims to prevent child abuse and neglect in all its forms and to give practical help to families with children at risk. The NSPCC also produces leaflets with information and advice on positive parenting – for these, call 020 7825 2500.

Parentline Plus

520 Highgate Studios
53–76 Highgate Road
Kentish Town
London NW5 1TL

Helpline: 0808 800 2222
Textphone: 0800 783 6783
Fax: 020 7284 5501
email: centraloffice@parentlineplus.
   org.uk

Website: www.parentlineplus.org.uk

Provides a freephone helpline and courses for parents via the Parent Network Service. Parentline Plus also includes the National Stepfamily Association. For all information, call the Parentline freephone number: 0808 800 2222.

Parents at Work
45 Beech Street
London EC2Y 8AD

Tel: 020 7628 3565
Fax: 020 7628 3591
email: info@parentsatwork.org.uk

Website: www.parentsatwork.org.uk

By working with parents and organisations alike, Parents at Work helps children, working parents and their employers to find a better balance between responsibilities at home and at work.

Parents Information Network (PIN)
PO Box 16394
London SE1 3ZP

Tel: 020 7357 9078
Fax: 020 7357 9077
email: editor@pin.org.uk

Website: www.pin-parents.com

Provides information and advice to parents whose children are using computers and the Internet.

Positive Parenting
2A South Street
Gosport
Hampshire PO12 1ES

Tel: 023 9252 8787
Fax: 023 9250 1111
email: info@parenting.org.uk

Websites: www.positiveparenting.info
www.parenting.org.uk

Positive Parenting is an organisation whose vision is to make training and support accessible to all parents within their community. It publishes a range of low-cost, easy-to-read, commonsense resource materials, and runs regular training days nationwide.

Relate
Herbert Gray College
Little Church Street
Rugby CV21 3AP

Tel: 01788 573 241
email: enquiries@national.relate.org.uk

Website: www.relate.org.uk

In Northern Ireland
Relate
76 Dublin Road
Belfast BT2 7HP

Tel: 028 9032 3454

Provides a confidential counselling service for relationship problems of any kind. Local branches are listed in the phone book.

Sure Start
Level 2
Caxton House

Tothill Street
London SW1H 9NA

Tel: 020 7273 4830
Fax: 020 7273 5182
e-mail: sure.start@dfee.gov.uk

Website: www.surestart.gov.uk (for information about existing local Sure Start programmes)

Sure Start is the government's programme to support children, parents and communities through the integration of early education, childcare and health and family support services.

Parenting courses

Parentalk Parenting Course
A video-based parenting course designed to give groups of mums and dads the opportunity to share their experiences, learn from each other and discover some principles of parenting. For more information, phone 020 7450 9073.

Positive Parenting
Responsible for running a range of parenting courses across the UK. For more information, phone 023 9252 8787.

Parent Network
For more information, call Parentline Plus on 0808 800 2222.

More about **Paren**$\dagger$alk

Launched in 1999, in response to research, which revealed that one in three parents feel like failures, Parentalk is all about inspiring parents to make the most of their vitally important role.

A registered charity, we exist to provide relevant information and advice for mums and dads in a format that they feel most comfortable with, regardless of their background or family circumstances.

Our current activities include:

The Parentalk Parenting Principles Course

Already used by almost 25,000 mums and dads, this video-based resource brings groups of parents together to share their experiences, laugh together and learn from one another. Filmed at the studios of GMTV, endorsed by the National Confederation of Parent–Teacher Associations and featuring

Parentalk founder Steve Chalke, the course is suitable for use by groups of parents in their own homes, schools, PTAs, pre-schools and nurseries, by health visitors at health centres or family centres, by employers, churches and other community groups.

Parentalk Local Events

Looking at every age group from the toddler to the teenage years, from How to Succeed as a Parent to How to Succeed as a Grandparent, Parentalk evenings are a specially tailored fun mixture of information, shared stories and advice for success as a mum or dad or grandparent. Operating across the country, the Parentalk team of speakers can also provide input on a range of more specialist subjects such as Helping Your Child Sleep, or Striking a Healthy Balance between Work and Family Life.

Parentalk at Work Events

Parentalk offer lunchtime and half-day workshops for employers and employees at their place of work, looking at getting the balance right between the responsibilities of work and those of a family. Parentalk also provides a life-coaching service for employees, helping them to deal with the pressures they encounter at home in order to be happier, and perform better, at work.

182

All Parentalk at Work initiatives are backed up by a comprehensive website: **www.parentalk.co.uk/atwork**

The Parentalk Guide Series

In addition to the How to Succeed Series, Parentalk offers a comprehensive series of titles looking at a wide variety of parenting issues. Easy to read, down to earth and full of practical information and advice.

The Parentalk Schools Pack

This resource, designed especially for Year 9 pupils, builds on the success of the Parentalk Video Course to provide material for eight lessons on subjects surrounding preparing for parenthood. The pack has been tailored to dovetail with the PHSE and citizenship curriculum and is available for teachers to download from the Parentalk website.

www.parentalk.co.uk

www.parentalk.co.uk is a lively upbeat site exclusively for parents, packed with fun ideas, practical advice and some great tips for making the most of being a mum or dad.

183

To find out more about any of these Parentalk initiatives, our plans for the future or to receive our quarterly newsletter, contact a member of the team at the address below:

Parentalk
115 Southwark Bridge Road
London
SE1 0AX

Tel: 020 7450 9073
Fax: 020 7450 9060
email: info@parentalk.co.uk

**Helping parents make the most of every stage
of their child's growing up.**

(Registered Charity No.: 1074790)